# Quieting Reform

# Quieting Reform

Social Science and Social Action
in an Urban Youth Program

ROBERT E. STAKE

University of Illinois Press
Urbana and Chicago

This case study was assisted by
Deborah Trumbull, Jennifer McCreadie,
Susan Hill, and Naomi Richmond

with manuscript work by
Colleen Frost and Melinda Clem

*This book is printed on acid-free paper.*

Library of Congress Cataloguing in Publication Data

Stake, Robert E.
   Quieting reform.

   Bibliography: p.
   Includes index.
   1. Socially handicapped youth—Education—United
States—Case studies.  2. Socially handicapped youth—
Rehabilitation—United States—Case studies.  3. Evalu-
ation research (Social action programs)—United States—
Case studies.  I. Title.
LC4091.S63   1986      371.96'7'0973      85-23221
ISBN 0-252-01232-1 (alk. paper)

# Contents

**Preface**             **ix**

**1**   **The Evaluation Study of Cities-in-Schools**      **3**
The Cities-in-Schools Program
Personalistic Youth Help
   A Continuing Appeal
Political and Bureaucratic Contexts
   Origins of the Program
   The Federal Period

**2**   **A Social Science Proposal and Technical Review**      **25**
The Evaluation Proposal
   Stakeholders
The Technical Review Panel
The Evaluation Design
   A Changing Sweep of Questions

**3**   **The Evaluation Work and the Evaluators' Dismay**      **45**
The Schedule
   Three High Schools
Staffing
Data Collection and Feedback
   Impact Data
   NIE Monitoring
Advice from the Technical Review Panel
   Issues
   Intervention

Discussion of *Final Report* Issues
    The Stakeholder Effort
The *Final Report*
    The *Final Report* Preparation Process
    The Findings
Subsequent Events

**4  Contrasting Views of the Evaluation Study**                        **99**
William Milliken and Other CIS People
Karl Kalp and Other Nonprogram Stakeholders
Robert Perloff and Other Technical Review Panelists

**5  The Evaluators' Accomplishment**                                   **129**
The Production of Knowledge
    Problem Reduction vs. Solution Building
    The Extension of Theory
Utility of the Study
    The Stakeholders
Enervating Improvement
    The Quieting That Occurred
    Knowing and Believing

**Bibliography**                                                        **165**

**Index**                                                              **169**

## Tables and Figures

*Tables*

 1  A Calendar of AIR Evaluation Project Activities and
    Events, 1977–81                                                                        xiv
 2  Enrollment and Staffing in CIS, 1978–79 and 1979–80          7
 3  Services Delivery and Integration in the AIR Evaluation
    Design                                                                                   37
 4  AIR Cost Categories                                                              39
 5  AIR-Estimated Full-Time-Equivalent Personnel for
    Evaluation Tasks                                                                52
 6  Full-Time-Equivalent Persons Assigned (For Pay Record
    Purposes) to the CIS Evaluation Study                            54
 7  Estimated FTE Personnel Needed and Actual FTE
    Persons Paid                                                                        55
 8  AIR Gross Summary of the Impact of CIS                          63
 9  Number of Days Students Were Absent                            65
10  Changes in Arrest and Probability of Rearrest                66
11  Chart of Student/Staff Member Agreement on the CIS
    Program                                                                              75

*Figures*

 1  The first page of the AIR *Final Report*                          10
 2  CIS national board of directors and contributors, 1979    14
 3  Excerpt from the *Washington Monthly*                        20
 4  Excerpt from the *New Republic*                                  22
 5  AIR basic program assessment model                          26
 6  A page from the AIR proposal showing emphasis on
    stakeholders                                                                        28
 7  AIR task schedule for the Cities-in-Schools evaluation   43
 8  Conclusions, AIR *Final Report*                                    92

# Preface

This is a case study; actually it is a case study of social scientists doing a case study. They were studying a program with the odd title of "Cities-in-Schools" (CIS). It involved some people trying to help several hundred severely disadvantaged ghetto youth in trouble—youngsters not behaving the ways teachers, officers of the law, and other members of society wanted them to. Jimmy and Rosalynn Carter got interested and secured quite a bit of government money for them. By government reckoning, it was necessary to have a formal evaluation study, to see if Cities-in-Schools was doing any good, to see if it should be supported in other cities. A research corporation, the American Institutes for Research (AIR), got additional government money to do a three-year study. That study ended in 1981.

Of course by 1981 the Carters were gone, the money was gone, the program was almost gone, and the youngsters still had pretty much the same problems—as did we all. It is not unusual to find that social problems survive our best remedial efforts, nor that we did not learn as much from the efforts as we expected. But it is unusual to become aware that the research is contributing to a feeling that perhaps reform is futile, that in some situations social research may be an enemy of reform.

This case study does not prove that social research is ever the enemy of reform. As did Ibsen's *An Enemy of the People*, it presents an instance where an idea needs to be considered. What I have done here is to examine the many pressures upon the evaluation researchers, noting the multiplicity of interests, the differences in perception of what constitutes success, and the increasing incompatibility between what the youthworkers see as progress and what the

evaluators count as impact. Even though aware of their organizational shortcomings, the Cities-in-Schools people felt increasingly
estranged and unrewarded for dogged, even valiant efforts. What
primarily resulted was not a greater wisdom about social services
but a lessening, a quieting, of reform.

## Methodological Notes

This case study of the evaluation of Cities-in-Schools was designed and carried out as a responsive-naturalistic study. It is "responsive" in that I concentrated largely on themes and issues
actually found in the work of the evaluators. I tried to orient to the
concerns and vulnerabilities of those who had a "stake" in the evaluation, hoping to add to their understanding of what happened. It is
"naturalistic" in that ordinary events, witnessing and documentation, are featured, not so much to instruct readers as to enable them
to add to their own experience.

This approach to educational research has been described by
Louis Smith (1978), Egon Guba (1978), and myself (1978). I probably
have been most influenced methodologically by the writings of Lee
Cronbach (see 1982), though I have taken some ideas to extremes he
has not sanctioned.

In recent years the case study approach has become increasingly popular in educational research. But many researchers object
to various aspects of case study as I did it here. Briefly in the paragraphs below I will try to identify and justify those aspects.

I have tried to emphasize the uniqueness of this case more than
its generality. I have paid less attention to what in this AIR work is
common to other evaluation studies, more to its special context and
meaning. Believing that each reader will generalize to sites and circumstances about which I know little, I have tried to provide great
detail about particulars that facilitate those reader-made generalizations. I have sought what Mary Kennedy calls "working
knowledge" (1982).

I have tried to tell the story in "their own words," using AIR and
CIS documents and quoting the people involved. The quotations and
descriptions herein are too long and too uninterpreted, especially for
readers who would like to be told just what it all means. Not all the
narrative "leads somewhere," but I hope it all helps portray the action and the context.

A special aspect of this particularization is my rather personal presentation. Most evaluation writers avoid emphasis on personalities. I examine them closely. Education and educational evaluation are greatly determined by spontaneity and intuition, and "the particular" cannot be well understood, I believe, without a personal dimension.

Most of my colleagues would grant anonymity to as many people, programs, and places as they could. Exposure often leads to undervaluing. To an important extent, personal detail such as I have provided is demeaning. I regret that. My model is not the journalistic exposé. Nevertheless, I have avoided pseudonyms because they limit a reader's opportunity to combine new information with that already held. And here, where millions in public money were spent for a small program, and three-quarters of a million more for the evaluation, arguments for privacy for key figures seem unpersuasive.

Perhaps the most objectionable feature of their case study is a pervading presence of the biases expressed above. In examining Charles Murray's work I have not been a dispassionate reviewer. Even in describing it, and certainly in interpreting it, I have applied *my* standards. I have noted other standards. I have tried to be fair. But I have not tried to eliminate subjectivity (see more of this argument in Stake, 1981). Rather, I have tried to make subjectivity more apparent. I have tried to remind the reader that my investigation, too, is personal.

What I am makes a difference that should not be masked. I have often been an advisor to the National Institute of Education (NIE) and would like to be in the future. I was an advisor to this AIR work. In the last year I have been an advisor to the possibly continuing CIS national program. I argued for responsive-naturalistic evaluation on those several occasions, and before and after, and am arguing for it again in this case study, both by example and indirectly in interpretation.

While writing this case study I have been the Director of the Center for Instructional Research and Curriculum Evaluation at the University of Illinois. I have been drawn by evaluation persuasions of my CIRCE colleagues, particularly Tom Hastings, Ernest House, and Terry Denny, and my doctoral students, particularly Oli Proppe, Judy Dawson, Naomi Richmond, Sue Hill, and Deborah Trumbull. We have been advocating an evaluation methodology that features interpreted experience, intuition, empathic understanding, intentionality, contextuality, and uniqueness of the individual case. In this review of Charles Murray's evaluation our advocacy surely has colored my vision.

Since Murray's work was largely completed before I began the study, I relied heavily on interviews and document review. For correction, validation, and further data collection I asked key interviewees to confirm what I was hearing from them and to react to what I was saying about them. With Charles Murray this required an inordinate amount of his time, which for months he gave generously.

Others who reacted to snippets and then to the whole manuscript were Norman Gold, Joyce McWilliams, Malcolm Klein, and Paul Schwarz. One who responded, Myrtice Taylor of the Atlanta schools, indicated that my quotations of Jarvis Barnes misrepresented the situation there. I changed the presentation a little but understand she still feels they are poorly represented in this book. This review procedure improved many passages, but was time-consuming and left many people at least a little aggravated. I grant that the complexity of their situations and the integrity of their commitments are not fully indicated.

Among others who made helpful suggestions for the final manuscript were Lee Cronbach, Richard Pring, Nick Smith, David Cohen, Deborah Rugg, Alan Peshkin, Gordon Hoke, Donald Hogben, Hallie Preskill, and Mima Spencer. Ernest House and Eleanor Farrar were working on a similar study at the time, and their reactions were especially useful.

House once wrote (1977) about the similarity between evaluation research and argumentation. I do not hope my readers will be instructed so much as I hope they will be persuaded. I also hope they will be aware that a fallible, sometimes contentious researcher observed the AIR evaluation and created this case study.

There are several stories told here. The main one is the story of the evaluation study. It is not meaningful without the story of the social services reform effort. Nor is it meaningful without descriptions of a community of evaluation researchers called upon for assistance. These in turn need explication of an evolving federal and political scene, with particular attention to the National Institute of Education.

One cannot tell all these stories effectively in a single chronology or make history simple by telling the stories separately. On numerous occasions I have sacrificed chronology to theme, and I beg the reader's tolerance with confusions in sequence. Also, I tell too little of the actual work with urban youth; it was pretty much completed before I began the metaevaluation. Table 1 should be of help in following the historical sequence, and the Contents can reorient the reader to issues and context. Such perplexities are not unusual for authors and readers of naturalistic research.

Asked why beyond personal reason I wanted these stories published, I have answered: I want readers to wonder if, in the context of human services, it may be possible for a well-reasoned social science orientation to work against, even while also working for, the public interest. The case of Cities-in-Schools provides a good opportunity to consider our evaluation work. I want to make this record available to evaluators and others so its issues may be studied.

Robert E. Stake

Table 1.  A Calendar of AIR Evaluation Project Activities and Events, 1977–81

| | EVALUATION PROJECT ACTUAL ACTIVITIES | EVENTS |
|---|---|---|
| 77 Jul | | Weiner paper on stakeholder evaluation |
| 77 Aug | | RFP for CIS evaluation appears |
| 77 Aug | | |
| 77 Sep | | School begins |
| 77 Sep | (Fieldwork continuing, on S & G Project) | AIR submits Technical Proposal to NIE |
| 77 Oct | Orientation to program; Review documents; | Evaluation contract begins |
| 77 Oct | Contact CIS personnel, district personnel; | |
| 77 Nov | Discuss data needs, data sources, access; | |
| 77 Nov | Prepare program descriptions; | |
| 77 Dec | Informal interaction with stakeholders; | |
| 77 Dec | Review documents; Set up data files | |
| 78 Jan | Organize stakeholder groups; Complete descriptions; | |
| 78 Jan | Assemble Tech Review Panel; | Tech Review Panel convenes, Indianapolis |
| 78 Feb | Distribute *Program Descriptions*, Rpt #1; | Report #1 is published |
| 78 Feb | Complete evaluation design; Meet stakeholders | National Stakeholder Mtg, White House |
| 78 Mar | Circulate draft of design; | Stakeholder meetings, New York, Atlanta |
| 78 Mar | Refine variable list; Consider data analyses | |
| 78 Apr | Develop instruments; | |
| 78 Apr | (Murray: Analysis, writing up S & G Project) | Tech Review Panel convenes, New Orleans |
| 78 May | Interviewing | *Evaluation Design* published |
| 78 May | | School ends |
| 78 Jun | Gather data on students; | (Data collection for UDIS follow-on begins) |

Table 1. (*continued*)

| | EVALUATION PROJECT<br>ACTUAL ACTIVITIES | EVENTS |
|---|---|---|
| 78 Jun | Estimate year's program effects; | |
| 78 Jul | Analyze program condition; Prepare graphics; | (Controversy over UDIS evaluation begins) |
| 78 Jul | Shift orientation from pretest to assistance; | |
| 78 Aug | Present initial feedback to CIS staffs | Tech Review Panel convenes, Asilomar |
| 78 Aug | | |
| 78 Sep | Fall pretest data gathering | School begins, first evaluation year |
| 78 Sep | Study program processes, criteria; | (Standards & Goals evaluation completed, Murray) |
| 78 Oct | Intensive interviews begin | |
| 78 Oct | | *New Republic* article appears |
| 78 Nov | "Hanging around" observation begins | |
| 78 Nov | | |
| 78 Dec | | (Write proposal for Push Excel) |
| 78 Dec | | |
| 79 Jan | Write *The Program and the Process*, Rpt #2 | (Field trip to Bangkok) |
| 79 Jan | | (Draft of UDIS follow-on begins) |
| 79 Feb | | (Push Excel Evaluation begins) |
| 79 Feb | | |
| 79 Mar | Circulate draft of Rpt #2; | Part of Tech Rev Panel meets USC |
| 79 Mar | | |
| 79 Apr | Reconsider role of evaluation; | |
| 79 Apr | | Confrontation with CIS staff |
| 79 May | Revise Rpt #2; | (Preparation of *Beyond Probation* manuscript) |
| 79 May | Spring posttest data gathering; | School ends, first evaluation year |
| 79 Jun | Discussions with CIS staff | Field trip to Bangkok |
| 79 Jun | Write the Progress Report | Report #2 published |
| 79 Jul | Hire new Assoc. Proj. Director, (Hersey) for analysis help | Murray appointed Chief Scientist |

Table 1. (*continued*)

| EVALUATION PROJECT ACTUAL ACTIVITIES | EVENTS |
|---|---|
| 79 Jul  Circulate draft of Progress Report | |
| 79 Aug | |
| 79 Aug  Discussions of Progress Report | |
| 79 Sep  Fall pretest data gathering; | School begins, second evaluation year |
| 79 Sep  Internal (AIR) review of project | Indianapolis teacher strike begins |
| 79 Oct  Prepare ERS presentation; | Evaluation Research Soc Mtg, Mpls |
| 79 Oct  Prepare memo for White House; | Indianapolis teacher strike ends |
| 79 Nov  Rearrange data files; Feedback data; | *Today Show* |
| 79 Nov  Write *Impact Report*, Rpt #3 | White House memo due |
| 79 Dec  Analyze data; Make field trips; | |
| 79 Dec  Redo snarfed computer holdings; | |
| 80 Jan  Review White House memo; Fix staffing problem; | |
| 80 Jan  Check stoppage of data flow in Atlanta | Analysis |
| 80 Feb  Complete draft of Rpt #3; Talk with CIS people; | (Draft of "Days in Court" begins) |
| 80 Feb  Internal (AIR) review of project; | (Draft of 1st Push Excel report begins) |
| 80 Mar  Circulate Rpt #3; Prepare for stakeholder mtgs; | |
| 80 Mar  Gather implementation data; | |
| 80 Apr  Prepare for fieldwork; Work on data problems; | (Write proposal to evaluate Youth Advocacy Prog.) |
| 80 Apr  Prepare for discussions with CIS staff; | |
| 80 May  Think through recidivism problem; | |
| 80 May  Spring posttest data gathering; | School ends, second evaluation year |
| 80 Jun  Confirm services delivery shortfall; | |

Table 1. (*continued*)

| EVALUATION PROJECT ACTUAL ACTIVITIES | EVENTS |
|---|---|
| 80 Jun Prepare for stakeholder meetings | Indianapolis stakeholder meeting |
| 80 Jul Await data processing; | |
| 80 Jul | |
| 80 Aug Prepare for stakeholder meetings; | |
| 80 Aug | |
| 80 Sep Make final revisions of Rpt #3 | |
| 80 Sep Draft *Final Report* | Evaluation project officially ends |
| 80 Oct Circulate draft of *Final Rpt* to Tech Panel; | Tech Review Panel meets, Chicago |
| 80 Oct | Report #3 published |
| 80 Nov Revise *Final Report* draft | ERS Annual meeting, Arlington |
| 80 Nov Circulate draft to CIS and stakeholders | Atlanta stakeholder meeting |
| 80 Dec Circulate draft to CIS and stakeholder groups; | |
| 80 Dec | |
| 81 Jan | |
| 81 Jan | |
| 81 Feb Get addendum statements for *Final Report* | CIS National Board Meeting |
| 81 Feb | Evaluation project spending ends |
| 81 Mar | |
| 81 Mar | |
| 81 Apr Finish final revision of *Final Report* | |
| 81 Apr | |
| 81 May | *Final Report* published |
| 81 May | |

# Quieting Reform

# 1

## The Evaluation Study of Cities-in-Schools

In October 1977 Charles Murray of the American Institutes for Research began a federally sponsored evaluation study of the Cities-in-Schools program in Atlanta, Indianapolis, and New York City. He believed that the CIS program had a good chance of coordinating youth services in each city and of drawing the most intransigent or estranged young people into ordinary, desirable educational and social behaviors. He further believed that his study would provide good evidence of CIS program success and failure—and additionally provide policy-relevant generalizations for program administrators in cities, school districts, and funding agencies across the country.

Three and a half years later a final draft of Murray's evaluation report was circulating among various "stakeholder" groups. The report said that the project had provided sustained face-to-face assistance to the most troubled youth of certain urban neighborhoods but had not succeeded in coordinating social service agencies, or in delivering an improved educational program, or in permanently uplifting the youth. Murray was able to say a lot about what went wrong. He even concluded that no such program could succeed given existing government regulation and the pressures of urban culture. He was unable to provide substantial documentation of how much work and how much good CIS had done, but he was certain that the Cities-in-Schools program had fallen far short of its promises.

The story of the evaluation of Cities-in-Schools is informative because it reveals not only the political nature of program evaluation (especially with an evaluation designed for "stakeholders") but

3

also the elusiveness of knowledge useful to educators and social planners. The story is unique in many ways but reflects on evaluation research generally.

Here was a program with noble intent. It would seek out the most troubled and troublesome youth in the most troubling neighborhoods, upgrade their schooling, keep them out of trouble, lay the groundwork for more productive lives. It had money and political clout. The Lilly Endowment had been one of many early sponsors, and later Jimmy Carter personally "found room" in the Executive Office Building for a national CIS office. Cities-in-Schools was not merely an educational program but a human service. Whatever these youth and their families needed, the program aspired to procure. Educational and social services integration was a major part of the plan.

The evaluation study itself was distinguished. It was undertaken by an eminent educational research group, the American Institutes for Research. Its conception began with Secretary of Health, Education and Welfare Joseph Califano and Director Patricia Graham of the National Institute of Education. It was considered important enough to justify a separate NIE contract for technical assistance from the Evaluation Research Society. Seeing the political issues, NIE's program spokesperson and monitor, Norman Gold, insisted on a "stakeholder approach" (see Chapter Two), a somewhat novel evaluation orientation.

AIR researchers found this expensive national program in a number of schools in the three cities. At the onset fewer than a thousand youngsters were enrolled. The program would lose and replace many of these youngsters. It would treat them individualistically in uncommon circumstances. Much of this special attention would limit the opportunity for quantitative data aggregation.

Both program and evaluation study were unique—but perhaps not more unique than any federally funded program and its evaluations.

As to ordinary features, there was the need for evaluation feedback for decisions that had to be made before the study was completed and the need to start the evaluation work before the program was ready to be evaluated. Such an evolving, organic character is common among the few social and educational programs which get formally evaluated. Attention to the contextual restraints and opportunities of each individual application of a general program was

needed here and is commonly recognized as necessary for understanding the workings and quality of innovative programs.

In the eyes of federal officials and applied social scientists,
Cities-in-Schools was a "demonstration" project. If its effectiveness,
productivity, and impact could be adequately documented, it would
be considered for expansion into other cities.[1]

## The Cities-in-Schools Program

Cities-in-Schools was a collection of urban "youthwork" projects. The first were started as street academies for school "drop-
outs" by Harold Oostdyk and William Milliken in New York City.
With slowly increasing support from corporations, philanthropic
foundations, and federal agencies—and with increasing tolerance
by school districts—the projects grew and multiplied. In different
circumstances each took on unique characteristics, but an ideology
was shared.

The goal was to find the most estranged youth of the urban
ghetto and to bring them into the mainstream of urban society—
ultimately to become educated and employed, legally respectable
and humane. According to the ideology, zealous staff members, most
of them "outstationed" from a city agency or institution, would work
intensively, "personalistically," with the youth. The many institutions and agencies of the city having responsibility for youth support
would be brought together, even in certain ways "integrated," to
work together on schoolgrounds. The design called for "families,"
often 40 students and four adults per family. The tasks of the day
would be academic, decided by the schools, mainly centered on reading skill improvement. But "family life" would be rich with the cultural, athletic, and social activities of ordinary schools. Inter-
personal communication and personal commitment were points of
emphasis.

Consider briefly one of the sites. In the autumn of 1978 at Atlanta's Smith High School Project Propinquity (the name Cities-in-

---

1. Indirectly this "metaevaluation" review of CIS program evaluation
also was funded by NIE. Part of a larger study of stakeholder evaluation
utility and productivity, my case study was supported through subcontract
with the Huron Institute. My collaborators in the larger work were Anthony Bryk, David Cohen, Eleanor Farrar, Ernest House, Grady McGonagill, Stephen Raudenbush, and Carol Weiss.

Schools was less used there), 98 ninth, tenth, and eleventh graders were assigned to three "families." Each of the students was enrolled in science, math, reading, English, and social studies, all taught by district teachers in rooms for CIS students only. Two program specialists arranged trips, tours, and speakers. During that quarter there were 75 "caseload outings" and 32 field trips, including a five-day camping trip to Alabama, programs at Halloween, and two plays, "The Wiz" and "Tambourines to Glory." Each case manager provided emotional and physical care, making referrals to social service agencies as needed. One-on-one counseling and tutoring were common.

The image conveyed abroad of the CIS student was sometimes "the rebellious youth." There were some, but passivity and deprivation were more common than contentiousness and villainy. Education and health problems were seen more than legal problems. A 14-year-old girl, a chronic absentee, came herself to one CIS office to ask for help. She had multiple physical disorders—eyes, skin, malnutrition, arrested maturation. Her parents also were in extremely bad health, and unreceptive. Her CIS caseworker visited her home (squalor was not an overstatement) at least once a week for an extended period—never gaining admittance. The caseworker arranged for medical care, tutoring, professional counseling, and got her a job at a nearby Burger King where she could eat with regularity. The caseworker later served as pallbearer at her father's funeral.

A "program" at each CIS site was developed to fit within school requirements, personal interests, and the cultural opportunities at hand. In a sense these were not "programs," sometimes merely collections of activities. They shared something of a common history, funding, and ethical standing, yet operated individualistically and rather spontaneously within the demands of school and other civic authorities. Once CIS became federally funded, it was decided that generally shared activities flowing from the common ideology should be evaluated. It was decided that Cities-in-Schools should be evaluated as a single program.[2]

2. Problems of treating evangelical movements as programs within federal guidelines are discussed more directly by Eleanor Farrar and Ernest House (1982) in a case study evaluation of Jesse Jackson's Project PUSH-to-Excellence.

Table 2. Enrollment and Staffing in CIS, 1978–79 and 1979–80

| CIS Components | Number of Caseload Students[a] | | Number of Caseworkers[b] | |
|---|---|---|---|---|
| | 1978–79 | 1979–80 | 1978–79 | 1979–80 |
| **ATLANTA** | | | | |
| Smith High School | 98 | 101 | 11 | 14 |
| Carver High School | 125 | 105 | 12 | 13 |
| Academy A | 110 | 96 | 11 | 8 |
| Academy B | 96 | 133 | 10 | 9 |
| Academy T | 100 | 163 | 10 | 8 |
| St. Luke's Academy | 90 | 88 | 9 | 8 |
| Craddock Elementary | 120 | 128 | 10 | 6 |
| Total | 739 | 814 | 73 | 66 |
| **INDIANAPOLIS** | | | | |
| Arsenal Tech High School (Plan A) | 643 | 634 | 65 | 53 |
| Arsenal Tech High School (Plan B) | 310 | 144 | 39 | 14[c] |
| Arlington High School | 60 | — | 6 | — |
| Crispus Attucks High School | 71 | — | 8 | — |
| Indy Prep | 29 | 36 | 5 | 6 |
| School No. 101 (Jr. High School) | 124 | — | 13 | — |
| School No. 26 (Junior High School) | 74 | 40 | 8 | 4 |
| School No. 45 (Elementary) | 74 | 71 | 12 | 7 |
| Total | 1,385 | 925 | 156 | 84 |
| **NEW YORK** | | | | |
| Julia Richman High School | 162 | 199 | 19 | 29 |
| IS-22 (Junior High School) | 120 | 134 | 22 | 19 |
| PS-125 (Elementary) | 80 | — | 6 | — |
| PS-180 (Elementary) | 60 | — | 3 | — |
| PS-53 (Elementary) | — | 70 | — | —[d] |
| Total | 422 | 403 | 50 | 48 |

Table 2. (*continued*)

| CIS Components | Number of Caseload Students[a] | | Number of Caseworkers[b] | |
|---|---|---|---|---|
| | 1978–79 | 1979–80 | 1978–79 | 1979–80 |
| HOUSTON | | | | |
| M.C. Williams Junior High School | — | 77 | — | 7 |
| OAKLAND | | | | |
| Hamilton Junior High School | — | 78 | — | 15 |
| WASHINGTON, D.C. | | | | |
| Terrell Jr. High School | — | 157 | — | 9 |

[a]The exact number of caseload students fluctuated from month to month. These figures represent approximate levels during the first semester.
[b]These figures do not include project directors and secretarial staff in 1979–80. Service staff who do not maintain caseloads are included only for the elementary and junior high programs.
[c]Represents those Plan B staff with specific caseloads only.
[d]Missing data

Source: *The National Evaluation of the Cities-in-Schools Program. Report No. 4, Final Report* (1981), p. 11.

Each city, each street academy, each family had its own history. The earliest projects were located in New York City, Atlanta, and Indianapolis. Gradually adaptations were set up at numerous schools. By 1979 the buildings, enrollment, and staffing in all CIS projects were as shown in Table 2.

What the program was and how it worked in the three cities are amply described in Charles Murray's evaluation reports. The page reproduced in Figure 1 was photocopied from the *Final Report*. Both style and content are indicative of the evaluation approach.

During the four years the evaluators' views of the program were well documented. The major evaluation reports were:

| REPORT | DATED | TITLE OF REPORT |
|---|---|---|
| 1 | February 1978 | *Program Descriptions* |
| – | May 1978 | *Evaluation Design* |

| 2 | May 1979 | *The Program and the Process* |
| 3 | October 1980 | *Program Impact* |
| 4 | 1981 | *Final Report* |

These reports made clear that CIS staff members were concentrating on the plight of their young people. It became apparent that building an organization, creating a philosophy, participating in a scientific study, and demonstrating for others elsewhere what *they* might do were not as important to that staff as being face-to-face with youngsters day-by-day. The three criteria emphasized by the evaluators were: improvement in reading, staying in school, and staying out of trouble with the police. These particular aims were important to the program people too.

## Personalistic Youth Help

The action differed from the rhetoric. In the field CIS was seen as a services delivery program more than a services coordination or demonstration program.[3] It was a program characterized by charismatic leaders and missionary zeal. William Milliken, one of the co-founders of Cities-in-Schools, spoke at great length about the commitments needed:

Out on the streets I came spiritually to believe that you find your life by giving it away. I didn't understand it because all my life my culture told me, "You're incomplete. You need one more thing." If you get one more thing you're still incomplete.

Spiritually, to say "you get your life by giving it away" goes contrary to the whole thing. I thought "if that is true, then the poorest ought to have the opportunity to give. I'm not doing them any good unless they have the opportunity to give." How do you create an environment where that happens? We got them in a small-enough environment, the first step, to get an eyeball-to-eyeball relationship, keep remembering their name, etc. But that is the beginning. I've thought about it so many times since. It sounds so simple—simplistic. It's not a simple process.

---

3. The Cities-in-Schools plan of action called for "an experiment leading to an integrated human service delivery system. . . . The Integrated System coordinates local institutional personnel into a new management configuration. This configuration is comprised of small units of multi-disciplined staff who deliver coordinated services to consolidated units of named service consumers on a consistent and personal basis" (Cities-in-Schools, 1977, p. 5).

# Chapter I.

## The Cities in Schools Program: A Primer

As the chapter's title suggests, this is an intro-
duction to Cities in Schools (CIS) for readers who are
unfamiliar with the program.  Others may proceed directly
to Chapter II without loss.

### CIS' PERCEPTION OF THE PROBLEM

CIS is a program to integrate the delivery of educational and social services to inner-city students, using
the school as a base of operations.  The problem that
motivated it is a familiar one.  As we put it in the
Evaluation Design:

> Despite all the programs, all the money,
> and all the people that have been aimed at
> the problems of inner-city youth, a very
> large proportion of those youth apparently
> remain stuck in a cycle of failure, with
> "failure" defined in the elementary terms
> of an adulthood of stunted personal develop-
> ment, or destructive social behavior, or
> chronic unemployment, perhaps addiction or
> jail.

CIS holds that current resource allocations would be
sufficient to meet the needs of youth, if the delivery
system were not fragmented and uncoordinated.  CIS con-
tends that the system's ineffectiveness is a function of
four defects:

- lack of coordination:  comprehensive
  needs cannot be met in one place; services are fragmented;

- lack of personalism:  since each "client"
  deals with many "providers," no personal
  relationships are developed;

Figure 1. The first page of the AIR *Final Report.*

Source: *The National Evaluation of the Cities-in-Schools Program. Report No. 4: Final Report*
(1981), p. 5.

I may have more skills, born in the right place or whatever—but internally, put me in that same situation, I could be that junkie, too. And I am a junkie of a different type.

What's the difference between the kids that make it and the kids that don't? I wonder whether it was the teacher or the socialworker or somebody else who broke through the hatred, the hostility, the anger, the mask. Sometimes the walls were too thick. That person didn't want you in. They were not going to let you in at any cost. The ones that did let you in found what *they* had to give. Then life began for them. Which meant that the only way that the young person could give something away is for that other person to know how to receive—not necessarily "help" them, but to receive. (Interviewed by Stake, Atlanta, May 1982).

As Charles Murray and other AIR evaluation planners saw it, the idea that drove the Cities-in-Schools program forward was: personal assistance drawing the youngsters into "investments." In order for CIS to have the opportunity to assist kids in investing (or "receiving," as Milliken put it), an elaborate promise of services integration evolved. This is how Murray once described the complexities of CIS. He was opening a meeting with his ERS Technical Review Panel[4]:

We are evaluating an effort which got its first federal funding in the '77–'78 school year, but which had been operating in different forms since 1970 when the street academies started in Atlanta, earlier actually with Bill Milliken and Harv Oostdyk in New York City. The actual Cities-in-Schools notion started in 1974–75 in Atlanta and Indianapolis. The only site we have watched since its beginning has been New York City, but even there a rudimentary program of sorts was at Julia Richman (high school) in '75 through '77. So it is wrong to think of this as a program designed and sprung full-blown as the evaluation started. It has a long history.

As I tried to suggest in the "issues paper" it came about because a couple of really impressive entrepreneurs, caring an awful lot about helping kids, seized on an idea they thought made sense. It was sort of "We want to help kids. What kind of structure can we come up with to serve that purpose?" It later took on a life of its own, institutionally, whereby you do whatever needs to be done to get the bucks.

You now have this huge variety of activities which all fall under the label of Cities-in-Schools. The reports you are looking at, #2 and #3, focus on one component we call the "pure form." But in Report #2 we do describe the street academies, the elementary school and the junior high school programs, the delinquency programs . . . After initial intention to evaluate all those things, we decided that would not be the intended evaluation study

---

4. Murray said these things more articulately, more formally, and in greater perspective in the *Final Report*. This informal statement indicates how things were being vocalized.

because most of those cases were ad hoc, put-some-folks-in-the-school, put-some-folks-in-the-street-academy, kinds of efforts. They did not have the distinctive character of CIS in its "pure form."

Pure form, to reiterate, is to consist ideally of a set of caseworkers having four different specialities: (1) the social service specialist, from, for example, a Department of Family and Children Service, who has lots of experience with the ways of bureaucracies, what the different municipal agencies are, and how you deal with them to get help; (2) the programmatic specialist, say from the Boy Scouts or the YMCA, who has skill in organizing trips, special events, athletic teams, drama groups, . . . (3) an educator, ideally a special education teacher, to deal with the kinds of educational problems these kids have, and remedial education in general; and (4) a youth worker, a street worker, someone who hangs out on corners, gets to know the kids, and does for them what needs to be done.

Each of these four would have a caseload of ten kids. With each kid they would develop what CIS called "personalism," a very close relation with both family and youngster. The caseworker was supposed to know what the family situation was in great detail. (Transcript, Chicago, 1980.)

The work of CIS was quite different in the three cities, and at different sites within them, and continued to evolve at each site. Indianapolis had the largest participation, with a high in 1978–79 of 643 students in "pure form" at Arsenal Tech and another 742 in variations at Arsenal and six other participating schools. That same year CIS in Atlanta worked with 739 students at two high schools, four street academies, and an elementary school. The CIS people in New York City listed 162 high school, 120 junior high, and 140 elementary school students. Approximately 280 caseworkers were made available to CIS in the three cities to work with 2,546 students that year.

## A Continuing Appeal

Across three long years, from 1978 to 1981, CIS project personnel tutored and counseled the youngsters and did the "streetwork." They appeared to win more admirers among business people and parents than among education and social service agency personnel. The programs grew larger, then cut back to concentrate on the more eligible youngsters.[5] They encountered management problems, particularly in coordination and continuity. They were obstructed by

---

5. At Arsenal Tech in Indianapolis, for example, it was finally decided that youngsters eligible for Tech 300 would be those with high absenteeism (some were out over 140 days of a 180-day year), who were below 5.9 grade level in reading, and who met Title XX poverty criteria.

the problems of education generally (such as an Indianapolis teachers' strike delaying fall opening two months), received increased national publicity, saw CIS offshoots begin in Houston, Oakland, and Washington, D.C., and faced disruptive delays in funding. The number of optimistic advocates of Cities-in-Schools appeared to diminish as all this happened.

In February 1981 (with the arrival of the Reagan people) the national coordinating staff lost its office space in the Old Executive Office Building. It continued its advocacies from Atlanta. Political and financial support was waning and internal problems were many, but the national board of directors showed no inclination to give up. (See Figure 2 for an excerpt from a CIS brochure identifying board and sponsors at one time.)

In late 1981, after the "demonstration" period was over, CIS programs in the three cities found dissimilar future prospects in their communities. In New York City people from the mayor's and chancellor's offices took little note of Murray's not-very-supportive evaluation report. They listened to the pleas of Milliken, CIS Board Chairman Howard Samuels, and the chancellor's consultant Ronald Edmonds, and, with city funds, contemplated a new and larger CIS operation in the Bronx. In Atlanta's Carver High School activities were at a standstill, but elsewhere in that city CIS continued modestly. The Indianapolis project started the fall 1981 term with but eight caseworkers and 80 students, all at Arsenal Tech. Federal funding essentially had ended.

But winter 1981 was not a winter of discontent for everyone. CIS Executive Vice-President Burton Chamberlain continued to find a few people in the new administration willing to listen. The "not evaluated" projects in Houston and Oakland were reputed to be vigorous, with credit regularly attributed to their superintendents. Not contemplating the demise of CIS, the national board of directors actually worried more about fending off bids from "fad followers." The board discouraged efforts to begin projects in new cities (with the possible exception of Chicago, whose Superintendent Ruth Love— the immediately previous superintendent at Oakland—was a member of the board).

During these years the Cities-in-Schools program had evolved from a small scattering of activities to a large but loose aggregate of projects. It had burst into fresh variations in a few additional places but diminished, at least temporarily, as federal funding diminished.

| BOARD OF DIRECTORS | CONTRIBUTORS | |
|---|---|---|
| **CHAIRMAN OF THE BOARD** | A&M Records | Houston Natural Gas |
| Howard J. Samuels | Ackerman and Company | Howard J. Samuels Enterprises |
| Former Undersecretary of Commerce. Business Consultant | Allen Foundation/Ivan Allen | Indianapolis Corporate |
| | Alpert, Lani | Community Council |
| **PRESIDENT** | American Lutheran Church | Johnson, George H. |
| William E. Milliken | American Mortgage Company | Johnson Properties |
| Cities in Schools, Inc. | American Standard | Johnson, William B. |
| | Anderson, Robert B. | Lilly Endowment |
| **CHAIRMAN OF THE FINANCE COMMITTEE** | Anncox Foundation | Lockheed Georgia Co. |
| Robert H. B. Baldwin | ARCA Foundation | Lubo Fund |
| President, Morgan Stanley & Co., Inc. | Armand Hammer Foundation | Marcussen, William M. |
| | Arthur Andersen & Company | Masco Corporation |
| | Atlanta Life Insurance | Mathilde and Arthur B. Krim |
| Smith Bagley | Atlantic Richfield Company | Foundation |
| President, ARCA Foundation | Atlantic Richfield Foundation | Metropolitan Foundation |
| Dr. Landrum R. Bolling | AT&T | of Atlanta |
| Chairman, Council on Foundations | Avon Foundation | Midwest Federal Bank |
| Dr. Ernest L. Boyer | Bagley, Smith | Milchem Corporation |
| President, Carnegie Foundation for Advancement of Teaching | Booth Ferris Foundation | Morgan Stanley & Company, Inc. |
| Daniel B. Burke | Burkitt Foundation | National Distributing Company |
| President, Capitol Cities Communications, Inc. | Capitol Cities Foundation | New York Telephone |
| Anne Cox Chambers | Carter and Associates | Occidental Petroleum |
| Ambassador to Belgium | Celanese Corporation | Patti Roberts International |
| James H. Davis | Central Banking System, | Outreach |
| President, The Institute for Transit Management, Inc. | Inc. of Oakland | Philip L. Graham Fund |
| Rosey Grier | Century Development Corporation | Portman Properties |
| President, Giant Step | Chambers, Anne Cox | Reynolds, Nancy |
| Wyatt H. Heard, Judge | Chevron U.S.A. | Rich Foundation |
| Texas District Court | Cooper Industries Foundation | Rock-Tenn Associates |
| George H. Johnson | Crown Zellerbach | Rutherford Oil Company |
| President, George H. Johnson Properties | Cullinan, Nina J. | Saint Luke's Episcopal Church |
| George K. Kennelly | Delta Airlines | of Atlanta |
| Assistant Vice-President, New York Telephone | DeWitt Wallace Fund | Saint Regis Paper Company |
| Dr. Ruth B. Love | Emory University | Sears, Roebuck and Company |
| Superintendent of Schools, Oakland Unified School District | Estee Lauder, Inc. | Shell Foundation |
| David Lewis | EXXON Company U.S.A. | Singer Company Foundation |
| President, Exodus, Inc. | Federal National Mortgage | Sony Corporation of America |
| William M. Marcussen | Association | Southern Bell |
| Vice-President, Atlantic Richfield Company | Finch, Alexander, Barnes, | Southwestern Bell |
| W. Bruce Spraggins | Rothchild and Paschal | Superior Oil Company |
| Cities in Schools | Fireman's Fund | Surdna Foundation |
| Stanley K. Stern | First National Bank of Atlanta | Templesman Foundation |
| Vice-President, Midwest National Bank | Florence and Harry English | Transco Industries |
| | Memorial Fund | Trust Company Bank |
| | Folger, Nolan, Fleming | Union Pacific Foundation |
| | and Douglas | United Texas Transmission |
| | Forbes Corporation | Vassar Woolley Foundation |
| | Ford Motor Company Fund | Vernon Foundation |
| | Forstman, Virginia | (Robert H. B. Baldwin) |
| | Fuqua Industries | Von Rugemer, Judith |
| | General Motors | Wald, Jeff and Helen Reddy |
| | Georgia Power Company | Walter Rich Memorial Fund |
| | Geraldine R. Dodge Foundation | Wardlaw Fund |
| | Hedco Foundation | Warner Communications, Inc. |
| | Hewlett Foundation | Watkins Christian Foundation |
| | Holiday Inns | Weintraub, Jerry |
| | Hooker Chemical | Woodward Fund |
| | Houston Junior League | Young & Rubicam Inc. |
| | Houston Lighting and | |
| | Power Company | |

This booklet was prepared as a public service by Ogilvy & Mather Inc.

Figure 2. CIS national board of directors and contributors, 1979.

Source: Cities-in-Schools promotion booklet (1979), p. 12.

Formal evaluation research on this program in the three original cities found little evidence of success. Generally, people interested in the program and in the problems it attacked showed little interest in the evaluation report. The remaining caseworkers and field managers were disheartened and did not presume that corrections and new vigor could come from studying it. One puzzling result was that many intelligent, responsible, caring people granted the correctness of the report and reiterated their faith in evaluation studies, but ignored the report's findings and recommendations. These results will be amplified in Chapters Three, Four, and Five after operation of the evaluation report is examined.

In the *Final Report* of the Cities-in-Schools evaluation study Charles Murray wrote: "If the question is 'Is the program *as it exists* a good investment of public funds?' the answer from the three sites that we examined is 'No.'" He went on to identify several unlikely but not impossible correctives.

In contrast, six months after circulation of the AIR *Final Report*, Howard Samuels, chairman of the CIS national board, told me, "The CIS concept has emerged as a sound basis for turning around urban education. It was administered poorly in the three cities, as the evaluation study showed. When managed by competent program directors and school administrators the program works, as is being shown in Houston and Oakland." Two years later, in mid-1983, Atlanta, New York City, Houston, and Washington appeared to have vigorous projects. New ones had opened in Los Angeles and Bethlehem. *State* plans were under consideration in North Carolina and Georgia. The national coordinating staff had dispersed, the office closing its doors in Atlanta, but Milliken was working to open a new office in Washington.

## Political and Bureaucratic Contexts

Throughout its growth from a single street academy in the midsixties to a 35-site ensemble over a decade later, Cities-in-Schools was a political idea fired by political energies. Yet the cynicism, influence peddling, and backroom dealing often imagined in politics were not prominent. The project was inspired by an apparently sincere passion for doing something much better for estranged youth. Mayor (later Senator) Lugar of Indianapolis, Governor (later President) Carter of Georgia, Secretary of Commerce (later gubernatorial candidate) Samuels of New York City, and Mayor Koch of New York City all bought the idea, worked for it, took political risks for it. They were sometimes accused of being naive about the problems of social disintegration and urban education, but in this matter they were not accused of political contrivance.

Admiration for the program itself was seldom as high as admiration for the men and women who promoted its enormous and perhaps futile work. Clearly, some school district and government staff members were not admirers. A few had favorite programs of their own for rescuing these youngsters, programs not likely to be well supported while CIS was "on line." One federal official reviewing CIS accomplishments at the time the evaluation study got underway called the program "schlock." Clearly, Jimmy and Rosalynn Carter wanted the program to succeed, and no doubt they wanted the evaluation study to authenticate that success. But at the same time certain educators, researchers, and officials had reason to want the evaluation study to show Cities-in-Schools to be a collection of empty promises.

Origins of the Program

The name "Cities-in-Schools" was coined in 1975 when "J. Walter Thompson, a well-known New York advertising agency, volunteered to prepare a brochure for the New York program and suggested that the programs in all three prototype cities be known by the same name" (p.11–31, Report 2 Draft).[6] Also in 1975, with support from the Lilly Endowment, William Milliken and Harold Oostdyk formed the Institutional Development Corporation (IDC), a not-for-profit company to coordinate funding and management of local projects they and their cohorts created in the several cities. IDC succeeded Youth Research International, a "Christian Organization" founded in 1966. The local projects continued to use local names such as "Project Propinquity" in Atlanta and "Tech 300" in Indianapolis.

The concept of propinquity—that social and educational resources for youth should be coordinated, personalized, and readily available—underlies the developments that culminated in the Atlanta Cities-in-Schools Pro-

---

6. A later brochure by the Ogilvy and Mather agency presented an image of integrated services with the photograph shown on the beginning pages. The classroom was at Julia Richman. The "student" was a model.

gram. Harlem streetworkers brought the concept to Atlanta. There propinquity became a reality, first in 1970, when the Atlanta Street Academies
were opened, and a year later when Exodus, Inc., was founded. (P. 17,
Report 2.)

As part of a pilot program in six cities, the U.S. Postal Service
funded these academies until 1972. Then

> . . . financial backing was obtained from the Law Enforcement Assis-
> tance Administration, the Atlanta Board of Education, and the Governor of
> Georgia, Jimmy Carter. . . .
> . . . School Board President Benjamin Mays and School Superintendent
> Alonzo Crim toured the street academies to determine how the Atlanta
> Public Schools could assist Exodus. The result was the first Atlanta in-
> school program, Project Propinquity, at Roosevelt High School. . . . In Feb-
> ruary, 1974, the St. Luke's Learning Center opened under the sponsorship of
> St. Luke's Episcopal Church, the Atlanta Board of Education, and Exodus.
> (P. 18, Report 2.)

In Indianapolis, in

> . . . 1968, Mayor Lugar, a former school board member, visited Bill Mil-
> liken's street academy in New York on a tour of alternative school programs
> for inner-city youth. Mayor Lugar was impressed by Milliken's work in
> Harlem and shared his commitment to schooling ghetto youth. Coinciden-
> tally, a meeting was set up with the Lilly Endowment that year. Charles
> Williams at Lilly had originally met Milliken and Harv Oostdyk in 1965
> through their affiliation with Young Life, a Christian youth-service organi-
> zation, and Lilly had subsequently awarded a large grant to the Harlem
> project. (P. 27, Report 2.)

These contacts led to a project in 1973 at Arsenal Technical High
School, which grew to large proportions even before federal funds arrived and before the AIR evaluation study was conceived.

The advocacy groups then were fourfold: (1) program origina-
tors led by IDC's Milliken; (2) government leaders, particularly
Mayor Lugar and Governor Carter; (3) members of the business
community and foundations; and (4) school leaders. Parent, teacher,
and streetworker advocacies were not apparent. Noticeably absent
among the movers and shakers were representatives of the social
service agencies whose services were to be improved. And noticeably
absent from CIS discussions and public statements was indication
that what was happening was experimental, a demonstration whose
results needed to be *measured* so that other cities could undertake
such programs with sound understanding of the benefits and problems. That point of view was introduced later by federal officials, a

technocratic concept and part of a justification of spending money in
a few places without spending it in others. The evaluation study was
an idea born out of "bureaucratic thinking," not out of interest—
political or otherwise—within the three cities.

## The Federal Period

In January, 1977, Jimmy Carter was inaugurated as president
of the United States. When he and his wife Rosalynn made their first
trip out of Washington, they went to New York City where they visited the United Nations and I.S. 22, Mott Intermediate School, a
Cities-in-Schools site.

That same February Milliken, Willoughby Walling, and Dean
Overman, all of CIS, were hired as federal consultants and officed
across the street from the White House in the Old Executive Office
Building. By the end of March they had prepared "An Integrated
System of Human Services Delivery," the document subsequently
used as the basis for federal financing of Cities-in-Schools.[7]

U.S. Secretary of Health, Education and Welfare Joseph Califano, to whom would fall responsibility for coordinating the federal
support, was less than enthusiastic about the undertaking but did
not oppose it. Perhaps recognizing its political vulnerability, he asked
numerous aides how CIS should be handled. One, Norman Gold, a
program evaluation specialist at the National Institute of Education
(NIE), saw the program as potentially of great interest to research
and service agency planners and urged a first-class evaluation study.
Patricia Graham, then director of NIE, a research institute still
seeking respect from Capitol Hill, saw the impending evaluation
study as one that would draw well upon the capabilities of her organization. She warned that if NIE did the evaluation, it would not be
a "whitewash." Several evaluation specialists in NIE saw the evaluation study as an opportunity to try out certain evaluation methods.
Califano and Gerald Bennett of HEW organized site visits[8] and the
review of documents, then formally assigned NIE to contract for an

---

7. This document, called the "Blue Book" inside CIS, was critically reviewed by one "outside evaluator" as simplistic and fraught with errors of
omission (p. 41, Field Evaluation Report).

8. Bennett's team found prospects that CIS would provide "more personalized attention directed toward a wider range of needs," but that costs
would probably be "vastly higher" (p. 5, memo of 3 March 1977 to Richard
Cotton).

evaluation study. Thus NIE became not only a home for the evaluation but a stakeholder in it as well, for NIE had something to both gain and lose. The study might change NIE's image, favorably or unfavorably. Federal financing of CIS projects was never an NIE responsibility. Responsibility for coordinating federal support was at first assigned to the Community Services Administration. Later it was passed to USOE's Urban Initiatives Office, whose director, Kathlyn Moses, became project administrator. When asked if the nature of the evaluation study was different from what it would have been had USOE commissioned the study, she said, "No." She added that evaluation studies of federal demonstration projects seldom look sufficiently at changed behavior patterns, settling too quickly on achievement test scores.

In some ways a negative evaluation report would serve some of these stakeholders better than a positive report. As mentioned earlier, there were competing urban-focused social services and educational programs, some developed more on scholarly research and some more effectively integrated into existing school or agency organization. In addition, a ring of credibility, even respectability, accompanies a negative evaluation report more than a positive one. Social scientists are trained to consider alternative approaches, yet with belief in but a single truth and a single *best* approach for applying social science to social problems. Great are the professional rewards for critical comparison and discovery of shortcoming.

Of course, the possibility existed that the evaluation study would be ignored. Such would be the case in 1978 with a private evaluation study of CIS undertaken for the Field Foundation for consideration of a funding request. A few people learned that it existed, few knew its findings. Written in November 1978 by Judy Austermiller, a sociologist working for the Norman Foundation, that evaluation report concluded negatively: "In summary, there is as yet little evidence to support IDC claims that the Cities-in-Schools program is a more effective social service delivery model or that it is creating positive effects in students. Without a consistent program model in operation in the three prototype cities, it is difficult to see the value of measured effects. Indeed, CIS seems to be creating its model at the same time that the federal government is evaluating it" (p. 43, Field Evaluation Report).

Austermiller analyzed organizational and fiscal issues extensively, providing much detail that Murray (later on) did not. Auster-

*This is Bill Milliken. He used to be an impoverished social activist in Atlanta.*

*This is Rosalynn Carter. As First Lady of Georgia she helped bail Milliken's program out. As First Lady of the United States she has taken a personal interest in helping Milliken go national with his program to help kids in ghetto schools.*

*This is Jimmy Carter. He wrote a letter to seven agency heads in the federal government asking them to help fund Milliken's program, and provided the program with a suite of federal offices next door to the White House.*

*This is Chip Carter. He works for Bill Milliken.*

Figure 3. Excerpt from Howie Kurtz, "How Chip Carter Got His New Job," *Washington*

# How Chip Carter Got His New Job

## by Howie Kurtz

A few years ago Bill Milliken was just another social activist, trying to raise some money to help ghetto students in Atlanta with their problems. An engaging man with an evangelical sense of mission, he carried his message to anyone who would listen—local businessmen, state oficials, philanthropists—but he had to scrounge for every dollar. His repeated efforts to pry some money loose from the federal government had, as late as November 1976, gotten virtually nowhere.

Then Jimmy Carter was elected President and everything changed for Bill Milliken. Milliken became friends with the President and the First Lady back in Georgia, when they were occupying the governor's mansion. The Carters helped bail out Milliken's Atlanta program, and since the 1976 election they have been at the center of an effort that has gotten Milliken $2.7

*Howie Kurtz is an investigative reporter for Jack Anderson.*

million in federal funds. He has launched major ventures in New York, Atlanta, and Indianapolis, and is planning to expand into seven more cities.

Many of the federal agencies who have recently funded Milliken were strongly opposed to helping a program they viewed as vague and unworkable. But according to reliable sources, high White House aides pressured several officials in the agencies into backing the program by insisting that President Carter was demanding their support. The pressure was sustained by a written plea from the President himself.

Milliken recently returned the favor by hiring the President's son, Chip, in a $26,500-a-year job in Washington. When Chip Carter got the job earlier this year, he had just returned to the White House from the family peanut farm in Plains, looking for work and trying to find himself, so the timing was fortuitous.

*Monthly* (June 1978): 11–15. (Reproduced by permission of the *Washington Monthly*.)

Bill Milliken, aged 38, was born and raised in Pittsburgh (a circumstance that led to his acquaintance with Zamias in Johnstown). During the 1960s and into 1970 he lived and worked in what he calls "the movement . . . on the streets" of Harlem and East Side New York. His special interest was helping poor, dropout children at or near high school age, mostly black. He conceived, organized, begged money and staff for "alternative schools" for such children, attempting to give them personal attention and motivation they could not get in the huge city school systems. His wife, now an ordained Episcopal priest, worked in a social welfare enterprise called Faith at Work. In 1970 Milliken despaired of accomplishing much in New York and moved to Georgia. In South Georgia, near the Carters' home in Plains, he met Clarence Jordan, founder of the famous biracial cooperative Koinonia and, Milliken says, "the greatest influence on my life." The Millikens did not meet the Carters then. In Atlanta Milliken organized and got some federal support for "postal schools," where dropout children got the personalized attention he believed essential. They also worked parttime in Atlanta post offices. The schools were about to lose their federal support when he heard that Georgia's governor, Jimmy Carter, might help him. "So I shaved and got me a suit and went to see him." Carter was interested in Milliken's ideas. But it was Jim Parham, the director of Georgia's Department of Human Resources, who helped directly with some state money. Parham would figure later and importantly in Milliken's and the Carters' relationship.

**R**uth Carter Stapleton, Jimmy's faith-healing sister, knew Mrs. Milliken from her labors with Faith at Work and had the Millikens to dinner with Governor and Mrs. Carter. Philip Alston, one of Carter's bigshot Atlanta friends and supporters, arranged another meeting. After the 1976 election and then after the inauguration, Rosalynn Carter had Milliken "write up a lot of stuff" about his ideas on how to personalize assistance to poor people, coordinate public and private activities in their behalf, and train federal, state and local officials and bureaucracies in the attitudes and methods, all aimed at breaking down huge impersonal systems into small personalized systems, that Milliken advocates. He had tried and failed to sell his ideas to welfare and educational bureaucracies during the Ford administration. Rosalynn made the difference in the Carter administration.

She put him up in the White House residence during visits to Washington. She had him given a White House pass. And she *told* budget director Bert Lance—Milliken's way of putting it—to get behind Milliken and

his ideas. Lance and Mrs. Carter accompanied Milliken to a meeting with company executives. Milliken asked them for money and support in the form of staff help and promises of jobs for people trained in Milliken programs. Lance urged the managers to give Milliken what he asked. Lance put Milliken on the OMB payroll as a consultant at $152.32 per working day. He was paid $13,098.50 for 86 working days between February 14 and August 31, 1977. He and a few other consultants were assigned OMB office space. Their assignment was to study the feasibility of federal support for "integrated human services delivery systems"—Milliken's kind of systems. Jim Parham, then on the White House staff and now a deputy assistant secretary at HEW, oversaw the study and now oversees the federal support that resulted from it. Something awkwardly called Cities in Schools, an experimental program for deprived children that has operated in Atlanta, Indianapolis and New York and is soon to operate in the District of Columbia, was allotted $2,203,000 in grants from six federal agencies in the 1978 budget, plus $560,000 from HEW and HUD to finance an outside contractor's evaluation of the program. Cities in Schools is in line for about $2.2 million in the pending 1979 budget.

Two young assignees from HEW and its Community Services Administration, Willoughby (Wib) Walling and Jane Hansen, have two small offices and a foyer in the Old EOB and answer "Cities in Schools" when their OMB telephone rings. They coordinate the getting and use of federal grants. Milliken until recently used the same suite for work in behalf of his non-profit Institutional Development Corporation, which subsists on private contributions and gets no federal money. IDC solicits federal grants for Cities in Schools and for the state and local activities associated with it. It pays Milliken $26,000 a year. Chip Carter worked for IDC last year and Milliken hoped that he'd take charge of a Cities in Schools operation in the District of Columbia. Chip quit the IDC staff after a magazine piece suggested that his job was a payoff for the federal grants. A friend and associate of Milliken's, Maurice Weir, opened a private Washington office for himself and Milliken before the *Post* story appeared and is setting up the District program.

Milliken expects to be visiting Washington about twice a week and to be staying at the White House. He still has his White House pass. It all goes to show, I'd say, what association with Jimmy and Rosalynn Carter can do for a good man and a good cause.

**John Osborne**

Figure 4. Excerpt from John Osborne's column in the *New Republic*, 14 October 1978. (Reproduced by permission of the *New Republic*.)

miller noted that the "federal commitment" for the five years FY77–FY81 was $7.7 million and that for 1978 private funds were being budgeted "to match" the federal allocation.[9] She found CIS money figures imprecise,[10] noting that Willoughby Walling, her principal data source, was unable to provide a general figure for 1977–78. She quoted Walling as saying, "That was what we're paying AIR a million dollars to find out" (p. 57, Field Evaluation Report). Austermiller's assessment[11] encouraged Murray to make further demands on CIS managers for program monitoring and correction. In Atlanta, Indianapolis, New York City, and Washington Austermiller's report had little effect.

Despite President Carter's involvement, actually very little public attention was drawn to Cities-in-Schools. A portion of a column by John Osborne in the *New Republic* (14 October 1978) is reprinted in Figure 3. A Howie Kurtz article in the June 1978 issue of the *Washington Monthly* (see Figure 4) told of Rosalynn Carter's arranging private audiences for Milliken with the Secretaries of Commerce, Labor, HUD and HEW. Director of the Budget Bert Lance hosted a White House breakfast meeting for CIS leaders, heads of several large foundations, and prominent businessmen. But the CIS project continued to be little recognized publicly and was "outimaged" by the subsequent advent of Jesse Jackson's project, PUSH/Excel. The context of CIS development was enormously political, and project funding from both private and public sectors was also enormously political.[12] Local opposition to CIS was sometimes voiced

---

9. The composite federal funding for Cities-in-Schools, according to Urban Initiatives Office figures, was:

FY 78 $2,336,853     FY 80 $2,850,000     Total $10,117,353
FY 79 $2,185,500     FY 81 $2,745,000

(Private communication from Kathlyn Moses, 19 May 1982.)

10. Austermiller perceived reluctance on the part of funders and project people to talk with her, "perhaps because of close Presidential connection." She had a sense that Murray and Milliken were philosophically in tune with each other, particularly as to the importance of getting on the inside, working with the sources of power (private communication, 9 February 1982).

11. Austermiller's evaluation may have "quieted" enthusiasm at the Field Foundation; no support was extended to CIS.

12. Federal funding emerged from at least six agencies, agencies which had no history of joint funding and which surely would not have joined in

cautiously, as if it might be in poor taste to have doubts about it. But what happened in classrooms and on playgrounds and what went on in the evaluation offices seldom reflected CIS's highly placed connections. By the time the final chapters were drafted, most of these connections had disappeared.

---

support of Cities-in-Schools had not the President called for it. The question of federal agency autonomy and responsibility was apparent. Should officials support the President's solution or promote solutions the agency's people have been devising? Some federal stakeholders—however politically aligned—would be hopeful for an early demise of this particular urban youth project. The AIR evaluation reports took note of such facts. CIS board members objected to acknowledgment of the political context. They objected particularly to explicit mention of the Carters (see Figures 6 and 7 in Chapter Two). They implied that such emphasis put future funding at risk.

# 2

## A Social Science Proposal and Technical Review

If American Institutes for Research were to win the bidding for the NIE contract, Charles Murray was the obvious Washington-based AIR person to direct the evaluation of CIS. But during the two weeks between receipt of the Request for Proposals (RFP) and proposal deadline he was "riding the rapids," i.e., vacationing in the West. Vice-President Robert Krug prepared the proposal. When NIE sent 15 follow-up questions to get clarification of the proposal, Krug got help first from Jane Schubert and later from Murray and AIR President Paul Schwarz. The proposal was submitted on 8 September 1977. The response to questions was submitted a mere 12 days later. By 20 October AIR had the contract; the evaluation study was underway.

In the following review of documents attention will be given to the concept of "stakeholder evaluation." Stakeholder-oriented program evaluation studies are intended to focus not only on the specified purposes of the program but also on the purposes and various concerns of stakeholders: teachers, parents, and others with vested interests.

### The Evaluation Proposal

In his presentation Krug wrote of AIR's 30 years of experience with program evaluation and program impact assessment, arguing

25

its main strength to be "the conceptual framework and methodology it brings to evaluation problems." Particularly he cited work done for the Job Corps, AID in Thailand, LEAA's Pilot Cities Program, and VISTA. The AIR approach was said to feature (1) a decision orientation; (2) a rationale of cause-and-effect relationships which identifies program components to be modified; and (3) an emphasis on objective, observable indicators of impact. The proposal promised a thorough description of the program detailing inputs, events, and activities. The dangers of too inflexible a design or too early a choice of criteria were noted: "the 'how' of any ambitious social change program almost invariably alters somewhat between the planning and operational phases."

Paul Schwarz's "incremental ethic"—the diligent search for small proximate movement toward announced distant goals—was apparent.[1] In a major professional statement, "Program Devaluation: Can the Experiment Reform?" Schwarz spoke of "impact-plus assessment," with data to be collected on gradual changes away from unwanted behavior and *added to* data needed for the more usual correlation studies of treatment and outcome variables. He spoke of the necessity for evaluators to seek knowledge for building future solutions (pp. 79, 86).

The language of AIR's proposal indicated no abandonment of the traditional research-and-development approach. It was a linear or blueprinted course of action that commits evaluators early to particular outcome variables and instrumentation. The AIR graphic in Figure 5 illustrated the approach

In a rather traditional applied social science vein, the proposal committed the evaluation team to search for useful output information, particularly in relationships among variables, with key dependent variables to be those recorded with instruments and aggregated for statistical analysis. "We expect to present unambiguous evidence of services received (measures of magnitude) over time and equally unambiguous evidence of attribution to program events" (p. III-14).

Little use, it said, would be made of attitude measurement. "This is not to question the reality of the internal states to which such terms refer, but to seriously question the validity of using ver-

---

1. Milliken's view essentially was acknowledged—that "these kids have 17 years of adversity behind them; it may take a decade to realize productivity."

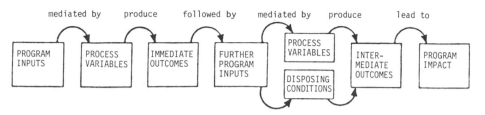

Figure 5. AIR basic program assessment model.

Source: AIR Technical Proposal, "Evaluation Designs for Cities-in-Schools" (1980), p. II-6.

bal reports of such states as indicators of subsequent behavior." It was implied that descriptions would concentrate on manifest overt behavior.

After stating a preference for unobtrusive measures the proposal authors made an interesting statement about quantitative and qualitative data: "For many dynamics, qualitative indicators are the methods of choice; and such qualitatively oriented approaches as the 'critical incident technique' rank among the methodologies we have found most effective. We make liberal use of the qualitative information, whenever indicated or required. But we do believe that an effort should be made to scale qualitative data after they have been collected, on some suitable quantitative dimension" (p. II-8). Thus in several respects the promise to provide thorough description of program activity and impact was conceptualized in terms of aggregated scalar data.

Citing earlier AIR work, different data sources were seen as differentially suitable for assessing action programs, with suitability highest at the top of the following list ("providing adequate validity is demonstrated"): (1) data presently available from routine reports, archives, etc.; (2) data potentially available, collected but not reported; (3) data from special directed observations or monitoring; (4) data from observation of responses to artificial situations; and (5) data collected through observer-client interactions (p. III-9) It was apparent later that, as planned, AIR evaluators did rely heavily on (1) above, particularly routine records gathered by the districts—to their ultimate dismay. Information of the lowest category (5) turned out to be greatly needed. From the beginning the NIE people called for a *stakeholder* approach, implying a need for observer-client interaction, though not necessarily for data collection in that

B.  Determining Stakeholder Evaluation Needs

This task will be conducted concurrently with the review and approval of the rationale, and will be based on the same set of interviews.

Our initial effort will be directed at the current use of evaluative information; who uses what, for what purpose. We will proceed to develop a conceptual map of the decision processes which characterize the Cities in Schools project in each city, and will begin to focus on the modes where better and/or more extensive evaluative information would seem to be most useful or impactful. In our view, previously noted, the value of evaluations are circumscribed by the decisions to which they contribute. By focusing on the locus of decisions, we are better able to determine where evaluation ought to be contributing to system improvement.

The next step is to develop a tentative matrix of evaluation needs for all major actors, from the hands-on staff member to the Federal level policy makers. For each entry, we would estimate the precision required of the data in order to satisfy the user requirement. A fine-grained analysis of client performance may be appropriate to a particular member of the project staff, but have no utility to the superintendent of schools. Too much information is as potentially damaging as too little; the objective should be to deliver precisely what is needed to each actor, when he can use it to some purpose.

The tentative matrix is then reviewed by each stakeholder. In the ongoing VISTA project, a rating scale was employed; each stakeholder rated how important a specified piece of information was, and what quality would be required of the data. In an Evaluation Needs Assessment project completed for LEAA in 1976, less formal procedures were employed in interviews with key actors in the system. In the Cities in Schools project we would propose to review the matrix with a small sample of stakeholders in an interview setting, and follow this with mail or telephone reviews by other key persons.

The final product will be a stakeholder-approved matrix of the requirements for evaluative information concerning Cities in Schools. As in the case of the rationale, we expect some uniqueness in each of the three sites.

C.  Determining Design Constraints

Figure 6. From the AIR proposal showing emphasis on stakeholders.

Source: AIR Technical Proposal, "Evaluation Designs for Cities-in-Schools" (1980), p. III-7.

way. Attention to stakeholders appeared in the pages of the proposal. One of those pages is reproduced as Figure 6.

### Stakeholders

The American Institutes for Research was not an enthusiastic advocate of stakeholder evaluation. NIE's strong supplication (in the RFP) for stakeholder attention was first acknowledged on the 20th page of the AIR proposal and treated as if it could be handled within ordinary information-processing operations. Prevalent was the perception of "stakeholders as information-receivers," i.e., as evaluation report audiences. This can be seen on that page, reproduced here in Figure 6. Note the emphasis there on stakeholders as people with information needs and as authentic contributors to the information matrix but not on stakeholders as potential collaborators in inquiry nor as potential victims of inequitable public policies and programs.

Subsequent sections of the proposal referred frequently to user needs for information and user assistance in determining certain evaluation questions. The proposal did not indicate that there might be difficulty in communicating with or understanding the needs of stakeholders.

Charles Murray and Jane Schubert in particular were aware of the importance of trust relationships among evaluators and program personnel—as emphasized, for example, by Brophy, Maisto, Burstein, and Chan (1977). AIR's evaluation design anticipated that the stakeholder emphasis would augment that trust.[2]

Attention to the particular meaning Murray, Krug, and Schwarz attached to the term "stakeholder" will reappear throughout this case study. The lay meaning of the term pertains more to having a share in the success and failure of the enterprise. When evaluator Ernest House heard the NIE-AIR definition, he protested, "The gov-

2. Much later, Norm Gold was to report retrospectively on the CIS fieldwork: "All participants had greater trust than is often the case. The trust endured over the life of the evaluation . . ." (1981, p. 22). But with multiple stakeholder audiences, contractual obligation to a federal office, and professional affiliations with the academic community, alliances between AIR and the CIS program staff were weak—as Brophy and his colleagues would have predicted. David Lewis and Burton Chamberlain of CIS (pp. 85–86) claimed that data gathering suffered because the staff did not sufficiently trust the evaluators. This all will be spelled out in Chapter Four.

ernment cannot be a stakeholder." House's point was that the government's stake crowds out the smaller stakeholders.

AIR's proposal authors had written that "the general constructs which will be used by AIR will differ little from the general constructs which would be used by any other evaluator" (p. 1, Proposal addendum). But Murray's use of the construct "stakeholder" *was* different. The term has more than one meaning. The proposal did not attend to alternatives. Charles Murray chose a particular unambiguous definition and stuck with it. Murray answered one of AIR's follow-up questions (#5) this way:

What is the general role of *Stakeholder* in this evaluation?

The practical application of evaluation results depend ultimately on the users. For Cities-in-Schools, the users represent an unusually broad range of individuals and groups. There are important stakeholders in the executive branch of the federal government and in state and local government agencies; in the community there are stakeholders in social service agencies, commercial enterprises, educational institutions, in neighborhood and consumer groups. Anticipating the needs and requirements of such a diverse population would be fool-hardy. The legitimate interests of these groups must be respected, and their unique contributions must be solicited by building in their active participation from the beginning, and continuing throughout the life of the project. For the evaluation to be truly useful, the stakeholders must provide leadership in the utilization of results. In order for this to occur, stakeholders must help in the establishment of requirements and priorities, review products, contribute to implementation plans, and offer ideas for dissemination activities. (p. 11, Addendum, Technical Proposal.)

Murray's words indicate his view of the stakeholder as an information facilitator and user. He declared that the stakeholder had a responsibility in assuring that information gathered would be useful.

Murray of course had no intention of involving every "important stakeholder in the executive branch," etc. It was not indicated in the proposal but later became apparent that, *for input*, a few stakeholders would represent others. For dissemination of major findings to individual stakeholders no special plan was put forward. Feedback would be provided to representatives and reports would be available to those who requested them. The active participation of stakeholder representatives was a strong assumption of the AIR proposal.

The degree to which information users were expected to be cognizant of and explicit about their needs for information was made even clearer in the response to another NIE question, this one about interaction with stakeholders:

. . . As more information is obtained, and the program rationale begins to take shape, the individual's role becomes increasingly precise; person A needs to know *where* in the math program students are having problems, while person B will make program-relevant decisions on the basis of certain cost data. This narrowing process continues; ultimately, each individual will be given a proposed checklist of information elements tailored to his or her particular role in the program. . . . each entry in the Data handbook will be keyed to the specific stakeholders who need the information, and the priority which was assigned to the need. (p. 15, Addendum, Technical Proposal.)

In actuality, the stakeholder effort never became so "tailored" (see the description of the stakeholder effort in the next chapter).

In covering the matter of stakeholders and many other topics the AIR proposal was informative, coherent, and comprehensible. Throughout, it exhibited considerable optimism about the forthcoming opportunity to discern quality of services integration and student remediation. At the same time it provided for feedback to the program staff for improving day-to-day activities. It implied that these activities should be governed by rational decision making and that reliable, relevant feedback would be welcomed.

As required by the RFP, the proposal said the first six months of the 36-month evaluation period would be devoted to preparing an evaluation design based primarily on (1) field study of the program in place; (2) evaluation needs of stakeholders; and (3) professional review of technical limitations.

The concept of evaluation services as information-providing predominated in this proposal, as it does in the thinking of most applied social scientists, professional people, and lay persons. The technical assistance role in formative evaluation, however, is often a matter of helping staff members improve their own evaluative review of program, to reconsider purview and priority as well as practice. Though this is sometimes accomplished by providing information, such noninformational techniques as those of the nondirective counselor, model builder, storyteller, literary critic, ombudsman, and cheerleader are not uncommon. The purposes of evaluation are recognized as political and advocative as well as strictly rational (House, 1977; Perloff, 1979; Weiss, 1981). Some evaluation specialists see these alternatives as stop-gap or unsavory evaluation roles, but such become part of almost every field study. Even though the RFPs seldom indicate evaluation purpose to be other than information delivery, to limit a proposal to this view probably increases the likelihood that the evaluation design will not effectively engage program operations.

Here, when the need for formative evaluation assistance drew AIR evaluators into less formal interactions with program people, they were drawn back to the task of producing generalizable information about the CIS "treatment." The correctives came in the form of review by AIR colleagues back at the office and advice from a Technical Review Panel that included research professors from social science departments of major universities. All were supportive of social services reform, and the social scientists had strong ideas of how reforms should occur.

### The Technical Review Panel

Originally, the RFP called for formation of an advisory panel to provide technical advice during the design and implementation phases of the study. The AIR proposal writers demurred, observing that "the Advisory Panel model has one serious weakness. The members of such panels are the subset of the 'best and busiest' who will agree to devote three days per year to the project. However conscientious and diligent they may be, they cannot deliver more than they promise; they simply don't have the time to get involved deeply enough to do what you'd really like them to do, and what you know they're capable of doing" (Proposal VI-8). AIR proposed review by an existing group such as the Stanford Evaluation Consortium or a university seminar on the design of evaluation studies. Marcia Guttentag, one of the NIE panelists for review of CIS evaluation proposals,[3] seized the idea and urged that the Evaluation Research Society, an interdisciplinary professional group of which she was president, be contracted to provide that service. NIE and ERS worked out such a contract.[4]

---

3. Other non-NIE members of the proposal review team were Willoughby Walling (CIS), Elizabeth Baltz (CIS), Helen Branch (Atlanta schools), and a person from HUD.
4. The NIE-ERS contract also called for presentations at professional

Professor Guttentag died shortly thereafter. Robert Perloff succeeded to the ERS presidency and, taking responsibility for the review contract, assembled the following panel[5]: Ward Edwards, quantitative psychologist, University of Southern California; Gene Glass, educational psychologist, University of Colorado; Malcolm Klein, sociologist, University of Southern California; Robert Perloff, industrial psychologist, University of Pittsburgh; Robert Stake, educational psychologist, University of Illinois; Eugene Webb, psychologist, Stanford University; and David Wiley, educational psychologist, Northwestern University. (Obviously this was not an existing group—such as AIR had advocated.) By the end of the second year the three educational psychologists were no longer participating.[6] For review of a first draft of the final report the group was expanded to include Timothy Brock, psychologist, Ohio State University; William Cooley, educational psychologist, University of Pittsburgh; Edys Quellmalz, educational psychologist, University of California at Los Angeles; and Lee Sechrest, psychologist, University of Michigan. The panel was convened three times the first year and once the final year: January 1978 meeting at Arsenal Tech High School, Indianapolis; April 1978 meeting in New Orleans; August 1978 meeting in California; and the October 1980 meeting in Chicago.

Usually such an advisory committee is formed giving representation to stakeholder groups. This AIR evaluation study was to have other ways of identifying pluralistic concerns and of monitoring the evaluation work to ensure that those concerns were honored. Here the Technical panel was to validate the evaluation strategy—not to monitor but to authenticate.[7] But, of course, members came with various concerns about urban education, criminal justice systems, integration of social services, the role of government in social af-

---

meetings and publication of monographs on stakeholder evaluation. One of these was *Evaluation Interventions: Pros and Cons*, edited by Robert Perloff, 1979.

5. Also originally invited were Kenneth Clark, Lee Cronbach, Richard Light, Peter Rossi, and Robert Schrank.

6. To join a team organized by the Huron Institute to study stakeholder evaluation for NIE, I resigned from the Technical Review Panel in April 1980 to do the specified case study of AIR evaluation of CIS.

7. Norman Gold noted also that in order for this study to be useful it would have to be perceived as having high technical quality. This panel would contribute to achievement of such quality.

fairs, the need for general knowledge for policy setting, and advocacies on how programs should be evaluated.[8] As will be shown, organizing such a panel changed the array of "stakeholdings" more toward having the study generate *new knowledge* about human services delivery and away from making the CIS projects as valuable as possible to targeted youth in Indianapolis, Atlanta, and New York City.

### The Evaluation Design

Norman Gold said, "Let's do what we can to make it the right study. Don't hew too close to the RFP line if that's not best."

As promised, Charles Murray distributed a draft[9] of an evaluation design to the CIS staff, the ERS Technical Review Panel, colleagues at AIR, and Gold at NIE. That was in March 1978. Murray had reviewed it in detail with Paul Schwarz, the project's senior internal reviewer, following a standard accountability and advisory arrangement within AIR. In April the Technical Review Panel met in New Orleans to discuss it with Murray and Gold. Many suggestions and comments were made during these two months, but none caused major revision. The *Evaluation Design* distributed in May was but a slight elaboration of the March draft.

The *Evaluation Design* was primarily a grand plan for measurement. The table of contents and the writing that followed indicated *the variables* needing to be recorded. Much of the selection was based on rationales for CIS work appearing in both its rhetoric and activity. A few variables were attributable to stakeholders responding to questions about their information needs.

With considerably more emphasis than in AIR's competitive proposal, this document indicated the AIR evaluation work would be an analysis of the measured *impact* of CIS.[10] However intermediate

---

8. Views of the Technical Review Panel role held by some of its members are presented in the next chapter. These members should also be thought of as stakeholders in the evaluation study—though not as stakeholders in the Cities-in-Schools program.

9. The authors of the *Evaluation Design* were Charles Murray, Robert Krug, Janice Redish, and Jane Schubert. Shortly after this report was printed, Krug and Schubert transferred to AIR's Palo Alto office and did not participate in the project thereafter.

10. Murray commented that the space devoted to impact partly re-

and incremental the study needed to be (because of time limitations, etc.), AIR would search for impact. It was implied that any assistance AIR should give CIS could be contained within its search for cause and effect. Process information, program treatments, critical incidents, and stories of key participants would be collected primarily to contribute to the ultimate understanding of what program components caused the successes and failures experienced.

During the previous six months of getting acquainted with program and sites, Murray, often with Norman Gold, met individually and in groups with various school, agency, program, "establishment," and parent stakeholders. Some conversations dwelt on information needed for continuation or expansion of funding. Many related to CIS promises to deal with outcast youngsters in a more holistic (some said "Christian") fashion, redeeming them to school and society. Not surprisingly, respondents more closely allied with education wondered about success in school. Those more closely allied with service agencies were concerned about success of youth coping with out-of-school problems. Those of the latter group were worried about the quality of services to be provided by CIS arrangements. The problems of program institutionalization in these cities and replication across the country held high priority for senior CIS people. Numerous groups, not least among them the national stakeholders, expressed a need for cost information.

Murray placed the information needs into four major categories and identified key observations for each. These variables are presented here in detail to indicate the way the evaluators talked about their inquiry. These were the four categories:

    I. *Impact on Youth*
        School-related outcomes
            attendance
            school achievement
            in-school behavior
        Delinquency-related outcomes
            self-reports
            police contacts
            court appearances
      Health, job, and other primary social-services problems

---

flected the greater explication needed to explain the technical aspects of impact measurement and analysis.

utilization of available services

Development outcomes[11]

    avoiding criminality, addiction, pregnancy,

        disdain of employment, and aggression

        basic cognitive, literacy, and social skills

        motivation and expectation

Treatment variable

    actual participation in CIS

    structure, activities of "the Family" (of 40)

Disposing conditions

    personal and family history

    city and school context

II. *Services Delivery and Integration*[12]

    Table 3 was presented in the *Evaluation Design*
    (p. 30) with the steps referring to elements of the
    CIS rationale, as paraphrased by AIR.

III. *Institutionalization, Intermediate Steps*

    Evidence of support by agency staff: e.g.,

        requests for assignment to CIS

        reports by seconded staff

        agency staff visits to CIS, etc.

    Evidence of support by head of agency: e.g.,

        quality of seconded staff

        visits to site by head

        endorsements of CIS within/outside agency

    Evidence of support by establishment: e.g.,

---

11. The *Evaluation Design* summarized one of two major thrusts of CIS as follows: "Despite all the programs, all the money, and all the people that have been aimed at the problems of inner city youth, a very large proportion of those youth apparently remain stuck in a cycle of failure, with 'failure' defined in the elementary terms of an adulthood of stunted personal development, or destructive social behavior, or chronic unemployment, perhaps addiction or jail. *If CIS is successful it will take some of the youth it works with out of this cycle.* The indicators of progress toward this goal will be called 'development outcomes'" (p. 6, *Evaluation Design*).

12. According to the CIS "Blue Book," the intended integrated human service delivery system would "coordinate [citywide] institutional personnel into a new management configuration. This configuration is comprised of small units of multi-disciplined staff who deliver coordinated services to consolidated units of named service consumers on a consistent and personal basis" (p. 5, as quoted in CIS Report 2, p. IV-1).

identification of active support network
editorials, features pro CIS
membership on advisory/stakeholder boards, etc.
Evidence of support by community
parent participation/support school activities
size of active volunteer pool
recommendations pro CIS to mayor, council, etc.

IV. *Cost Information*

The discussion of cost information was summarized by
Murray as shown in Table 4.

Table 3. Services Delivery and Integration in the AIR Evaluation Design

| Step | Assessment Indicator | Data Source |
|------|---------------------|-------------|
| 1 | 1.1 staff coverage | employment records |
| 2 | 2.1 staff qualification for position<br>2.2 professional mixture of family<br>2.3 continuity | resumes<br>resumes<br>employment records |
| 3 | 3.1 continuity of caseload<br>3.2 intra-family support | caseload rosters<br>staff interviews, contact forms |
| 4 | 4.1 amount/type/outcome of service provided<br>4.2 additional services sought by staff<br>4.3 information seeking by staff | interviews, contact forms<br>time-use studies<br>interviews, case files<br>interviews, case files |
| 5 | 5.1 number of contacts<br>5.2 time spent on contacts | interviews, contact forms<br>case files, time samples |
| 6 | 6.1 settings of contacts | interviews, contact forms, case files, times samples |
| 7 | 7.1 staff information exchange | interviews, contact forms |
| 8 | 8.1 knowledge of client, history and current status | interviews, case files, contact forms |
| 9 | 9.1 staff perception of client (time series)<br>9.2 client perception of staff (time series) | interviews, structured observations, case files |

Table 3. (*continued*)

| Step | Assessment Indicator | Data Source |
|------|----------------------|-------------|
| 10 | 10.1 home visits, number, frequency, nature | interviews, home visit reports, contact forms |
|    | 10.2 other contacts with parents, siblings, initiated by staff, or by parent, sibling | interviews, contact forms, case files |
|    | 10.3 family involvement with school | interviews, logs |
| 11 | 11.1 knowledge of neighborhood characteristics | interviews |
|    | 11.2 contacts with residents, merchants in neighborhood; staff or neighborhood initiated | interviews, logs |
| 12 | 12.1 services provided for family (amount, type, for whom, outcome) | interviews, contact forms case files |
|    | 12.2 evidence of client involvement in planning | interviews, contact forms |
|    | 13   (part of institutionalization; see Section IV) | |

Source: *The National Evaluation of the Cities-in-Schools Program: Evaluation Design*, Table 3.1 Data sources for the elements in the services delivery rationale (1978), p. 30.

The length of the above list, as well as its technical nature, became increasingly worrisome to CIS program people. Early on, they had been hopeful that the evaluation data could be obtained "unobtrusively," i.e., without being distractive to their work. Later on, not only was their attention required, but the staff became obligated to think of their work in the evaluator's language, this language of "variables."

On several occasions we colleagues on the Technical Review Panel considered this elaborate list of variables. We seldom suggested that important things might have been omitted. We sometimes indicated that as the activities got complicated and time ran short, essential concerns might be neglected. Occasionally two or three of us chided Murray for his psychometric inclinations or for seeming to aspire to create exhaustive management-information

Table 4. AIR Cost Categories

| SSC: Site-Specific Costs by city (actual out-of-pocket expenses in the three cities) | PCC: Project-Comparable Costs (same cost categories, with a standard dollar value assigned to each, regardless of out-of-pocket expenses)* |
|---|---|
| DEVELOPMENT | • IDC's staff and support costs prior to decision to implement by each site. City's investment in meetings with IDC, planning sessions, costs of tours of existing programs.** |
| ACQUISITION | • Development of materials, evaluation design.** Equipment purchase and installation. One-time materials and supplies. Pre-service training. Facilities. Orientation, coordination with non-CIS elements. |
| OPERATIONS | • DIRECT CIS COSTS: Project direction. Evaluation.** Management Support.** Salaries and benefits of CIS staff (direct hire and seconded). In-service training. Materials and supplies. Equipment replacement and maintenance. Contracted services (exclude if donated, for SSC). <br> • INDIRECT CIS COSTS:*** Transportation. Agency services that would not otherwise have been provided. School system services and materials over and above normal program costs. School system liaison personnel. School system facilities diverted to CIS use. |

*This does not exclude the alternative of specifying certain types of expenses that are expected to be donated rather than purchased, as part of the CIS standard operating procedure.
**The PCC can be expected to be lower than the SSC on these items, because of economies resulting from increased experience and knowledge.
***CIS should also add to the service delivery costs of other agencies simply by increasing the proportion of eligible people who get the standard services. But these are costs that the existing agency "should" be incurring anyway. The incremental cost of CIS in this regard will be noted separately from the incremental costs resulting from expansion of scope of service types or eligible clients.

Source: *The National Evaluation of the Cities-in-Schools Program: Evaluation Design*, p. 45.

systems.[13] It was sometimes suggested that specific CIS problems might not get studied. Murray would show such curiosity about those problems and such sophistication in relating them to previous policy research (some of it patterned on regression analyses like his own) that the criticism waned. Left to his own devices—as he himself put it—he tended "to regress to his own mean, stressing the quantitative aspects of the analysis."

Contact with field operations and stakeholders during that first six months could have expanded the data plan or simplified it, especially as costs and obstacles became clearer. The list did not get shorter. The evaluation project ideology grew more quantitative and technical, undamped by discouraging reminders of previous educational research in such urban sites. Illustrative of the ideology was deletion of the following sentence, which appeared in the draft but not in the actual *Evaluation Design*: "Each student's encounter with the Cities-in-Schools program is unique, and, in that sense, the 'independent variable' as represented by CIS may be characterized in as many ways as there are students" (p. 11, *Evaluation Design* draft). The statement replacing it in the final version read: "The second perspective on the independent variable will disaggregate the 'treatment' variable into a limited number of structural variables of interest to the replication issue" (p. 19, *Evaluation Design*). The statement concluded that "these analyses will employ multi-variate regression models of the form . . ." (p. 20, *Evaluation Design*).

There was little indication that stakeholders wanted information processing of that kind, but without doubt they would have said they wanted the most precise and valid conclusions possible. From Murray's perspective, the hard-data analytic techniques would be to his benefit in reaching the most insightful conclusions. He then would (he expected) convert any esoteric analyses into clear prose for the stakeholders. The *Evaluation Design* said nothing of apprehension that the measurements needed for these analyses might not be obtainable. At all sites Murray heard inspired accounts of the exhaustiveness and retrievability of the school systems' data. Un-

---

13. The reader should know that for a long time I have been identified as an advocate of making evaluation research more naturalistic and experiential, more in the style of the humanities and less like the quantitative social sciences. As much as anyone else on the Technical Review Panel, I urged Murray to rely on narrative descriptions more and on multivariate analysis less.

wisely he believed them. By and large the measurements were not delivered.[14]

## A Changing Sweep of Questions

The AIR evaluation team did not appear to use that six-month design period to make its plan simpler, more practically useful, or more grounded in the workings of CIS field personnel. Little in the *Evaluation Design* was historical, political, or theoretical. Yet there were frequent reminders that AIR had people of experience and talent for dealing with difficult social and educational issues. For example, AIR member Janice Redish's review of the human services integration movement in the United States since 1960 prompted the following section on "Service Delivery and Integration":

There are aspects of this project that are similar to past attempts at services integration (the case management, case team approach). There are features that are unique (location within the school system, the variety of services encompassed). Our assessment of the service delivery efforts will enable us to make statements about the effectiveness of these features that could be compared to evaluations of other service integration projects.

In addition, there are further questions that are of interest to agency stakeholders. In particular, they want to know: To what extent is CIS providing new services not otherwise available to these people? To what extent does CIS provide services that are available elsewhere (although in a different delivery mode)? If the services are otherwise available, to what extent is CIS bringing new clients into the system who were not already being served?

Answers to these questions are relevant to the ability of the system to reallocate its resources to absorb CIS. We will use interviews with agency personnel, case files, school archives to answer these questions.

And, far from least, we must address some extremely pertinent political and organizational issues. How, in reality, is it possible to tinker with bureaucratic networks and customs that are familiar, have their own virtues, and whatever else, certainly have solidly entrenched constituencies? But this question is better discussed as an aspect of institutionalization, to which we now turn. (p. 32, *Evaluation Design*.)

Instead of becoming simpler and clearer the evaluation design became more complicated and diffuse during the six months. According to Charles Murray, three pressures contributed:

---

14. The CIS evaluation contracting was unusual. Separate additional contracts for data collection were awarded by NIE to each of the three urban districts. This contributed to the optimism within AIR that good data files would be accessible.

1. The stakeholders did not focus on a few critical issues. They contributed a laundry-list of topics, each of which was said to be important to someone.
2. The CIS program staff wanted to evaluate everything—all the different components from the elementary schools to the street academies, Plan B to "pure form."
3. NIE's evaluation monitor, Norman Gold, encouraged both of the above. For him, the CIS evaluation study was to be a success, a landmark in his career. His inclination way to say "yes" to all requests, except those from the evaluators to trim back the evaluation task.[15] (Personal communication, 1982)

After reading my draft of this chapter, Charles Murray composed the following paragraph, in third person, overcritically describing his own management of the research study. I include it here without his explicit permission:

The person in a position to have fought these pressures was Murray, but he did not. Temperamentally, he preferred loose, broad-ranging data collection plans over tightly specified ones. Managerially, he tended to ignore logistical details and failed to think through the implications of the design he was proposing. But the real problem was Murray's perception of what was in it for him. Throughout the design phase, he continued to view CIS as the apotheosis of intensive service-delivery as a means of dealing with the problems of inner-city youth. He did not expect the program to be a uniform success. He did think it would provide him with a rich data base from which he would tease the dynamics that would make him, if not rich and famous, at least less obscure. He was the kid in the candy store. Far from simplifying, he kept opening new jars. Many of which turned out to be cans of worms. (December 1981.)

To an extent Murrays' self-criticism was valid. But it is important to consider it and especially the design against the ordinary and usual in contemporary program evaluation practice. The evaluation plan was overly ambitious and perhaps overly mechanical— but it was consistent with the advice of its Technical Review Panel and admirable in the eyes of most contemporaries. It was a plan most educational researchers and social scientists would today consider optimum for achieving explanation and understanding. As a plan and in its early deployment, the evaluation study of Cities-in-Schools was perceived to be "the state of the art."

It occurred to Murray that the Cities-in-Schools program might

---

15. Gold objected to Murray's criticism above, saying particularly that he felt the variations of CIS programs should receive much less attention than "pure forms" (personal communication, 21 September 1982).

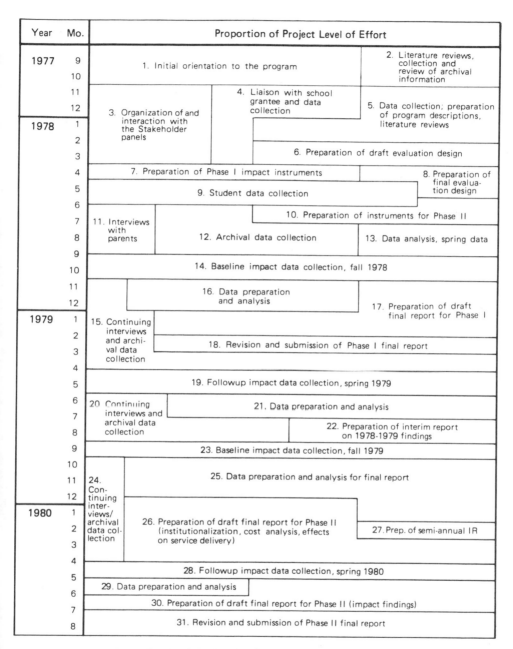

Figure 7. AIR task schedule for the Cities-in-Schools evaluation.

Source: *The National Evaluation of the Cities-in-Schools Program: Evaluation Design* (1978), p. 54.

not be ready for evaluation. He raised the possibility with Gold, with his evaluation advisors, and with his boss. The fact that counted was the fact that CIS was receiving unprecedented federal support to provide a service. As an audit, the evaluation study had to occur immediately. Long-term program development and social research might have made more sense, but "evaluability" (to use Wholey's term) was not seen as a criterion for going ahead.[16]

The *Evaluation Design* closed with an "Implementation Plan" which included a "Task Schedule." This proposed schedule (Figure 7) and the calendar of *actual* evaluation activities (Table 1) should be useful in following the description of activities in the next chapter.

---

16. The most pertinent entry in the *Standards for Evaluations of Educational Programs, Projects, and Materials* is the standard, "the object of the evaluation should be sufficiently examined, so that the form of the object being considered in the evaluation can be clearly identified" (Joint Committee, p. 99). Murray did that but did not assure that the program was suitably developed for the AIR research design.

# 3

## The Evaluation Work and The Evaluators' Dismay

The evaluation study began with spirit and high purpose. Three years later—to put the story in a nutshell—the study was slowly being concluded, with discouragement and with uncertainty. A common feeling among research-oriented evaluators was that the "CIS idea" had not had a fair trial: therefore the evaluation study had no critical role other than to state that fact. Observers oriented more to formative evaluation felt that AIR had helped improve program management and that the evaluation report would complete AIR's contractual responsibility by telling how well the problems had been overcome.

*Amid many obstacles, endlessly buffeted, the CIS program had matured—somewhat as people do: intuitively, with character, with vast unexpected encounter, with daily mishap and satisfaction—all with little of the heroic accomplishment once dreamed and publicly advertised.*

The evaluation study could not remain outside the program's troubles. The program experienced funding delays, a teachers' strike, confusing regulations, turf disputes, problems with untrained caseworkers, and management priorities unacceptable to various constituencies. The evaluators had encountered these obstacles before, but somehow were optimistic that with careful planning, abundant funding, systematic operational review, fallback positions, etc., "this time it would be different." It was not.

The evaluators redirected some of their effort to assist program development. They did not depart from the original intention to con-

45

ceptualize the inquiry around prespecified impact variables. Program problem solving was to be assisted but not studied. Evaluation assistants working closest at hand were not instructed that "the story" was to be carefully documented. AIR colleagues who understood the value of a "naturalistic" reporting of the evolving youth assistance work were otherwise engaged. True to original plan and design, AIR evaluators remained committed to a data collection they ultimately could not obtain and to issues they could not examine. The story they finally told—an accurate and relevant but incomplete story—was potentially useful to decision-maker stakeholders. The process part of the story was based, unfortunately, on casual experience rather than on the systematic data gathering expected of ethnographers, phenomenologists, and historians.

**The Schedule**

Even while preparing the *Evaluation Design*, Charles Murray deployed a junior fieldworker to each of the three sites to become acquainted with ongoing activities, to interact with school and agency personnel, and to make general arrangements for the collection of data. Based mostly on program documents, the evaluators published in February their first report, *Program Descriptions*, even before publishing the *Evaluation Design* in May.

Frequently accompanied by Norman Gold, Charles Murray met with many stakeholder groups in the three cities. At a February 1978 "decision-maker stakeholders" meeting in Atlanta's Peachtree Plaza Hotel, AIR inquiries about outcome information needs revealed stakeholder agreement in placing "highest priority on measuring outcomes displayed by students and their parents—both school-related and nonschool-related; especially student participation in neighborhood and extra-curricular activities and parent knowledge of available services and obtaining/maintaining better jobs (Minutes of the meeting)." Stakeholders attending suggested the AIR list be augmented by adding "items related to the absence of negative factors—teenage pregnancy, drug abuse, and alcoholism."

The early moments of the evaluation study were also spent in conventional ways: arranging access to buildings and files, developing instruments, consulting various specialists, and making commitments (e.g., for typing, computers, contracts) within AIR for the anticipated work. Because NIE created a special obligation to an external Technical Review Panel, unusual attention, and perhaps reliance, was placed on collegial dialogue for planning and idea development.

By the end of spring 1978—ending the first of the three program years being evaluated—it was clear that program operations were slow to settle into a routine; that operations at different sites (within as well as across cities) were greatly different; that the criteria for student admission were inconsistent with original intentions; and that obtaining impact data would be difficult.

More generally, the program that we were evaluating was not the one described in the *Proposal*, but a collection of disparate activities in inner-city high schools, grade schools, middle schools, and street academies. Some of these activities were undoubtedly useful. Some bore a resemblance to the activities planned for the program. But in no sense was the evaluation going to be able to assess the validity of the CIS concept. The concept was not being tested. (P. 34, *Final Report*.)

The problems Murray's people perceived were discussed with CIS personnel, with NIE people, with ERS researchers, and with AIR colleagues. The question often was raised, "How much should the evaluators press the program to return to original plans?"[1] The evaluators did point out CIS shortcomings and did press for "reform" of the reform efforts. And CIS voices (especially Milliken) responded. "Part of the CIS staff's response was that the evaluators had not asked the right questions, or that the Caseworkers and students had not responded accurately. But another part of the response was to try to make the program work better the next year. A number of steps were taken to specify guidelines for Caseworker responsibilities and to arrive at explicit statements of what CIS was supposed to be" (p. 34, *Final Report*).

CIS President William Milliken acknowledged that CIS needed

---

1. The role of evaluators as technical assistants continues to be debated in professional circles. It is apparent that evaluators have valuable experience with certain matters, sometimes knowing aspects of the program more intimately than program administrators do. Evaluator advice might be useful. It could be unethical to withhold it. On the other hand, evaluators are not fully acquainted with the sociopolitical contexts of the program. They have somewhat different views—not necessarily better—from those of program administrators as to what the program should accomplish. And once they have given advice they are not in as independent a position for further evaluating. (See Scriven, 1974, pp. 65–72; Smith, 1979, p. 206.)

improvements in the training of caseworkers and better record keeping. At Arsenal Tech High School (Indianapolis) with Elizabeth Baltz newly in charge, the second evaluation year commenced with an improved information keeping system and a constraint on admission of youngsters needing only educational aid. The evaluators increasingly focused on this largest of the sites, considering the program at Tech closest to what CIS called its "pure form."

Three High Schools

In Atlanta the long-standing but still unroutinized CIS street academies became exempt from AIR attention. Focus was directed primarily to Smith High School, where the project was more or less in "pure form." The Atlanta Superintendent of Schools had supported the CIS program in the beginning, but few APS staff people had taken interest. Individual sites had been allowed to operate pretty much as their resources and intuitions dictated. In New York City evaluation focused on Julia Richman High School in Manhattan, even though a large program was underway at I.S. 22, a junior high in the Bronx.[2] None of the AIR reports explained why the street academies and other schools were dropped from scrutiny. But Murray felt, and Gold concurred, that the evaluation resources should be concentrated in places where the original CIS concept (with its strong emphasis on services integration and assistance to the most troubled youth) remained relatively unchanged and where there were expectations of good access to AIR evaluators for data gathering and to data already gathered by the school district. (See Table 2 for roster of schools.)

The first full year of field evaluation (1978–79, actually the second year of the evaluation contract) went smoothly and productively for both program and evaluation personnel at Arsenal Tech. "Families" of 40 students and four caseworkers each were successfully engaged in tutorial, extracurricular, and other personal services with high *esprit de corps* and with good support from building and national program administrators. Reading scores improved. Absen-

---

2. In a highly publicized visit in early 1977 Rosalynn Carter expressed support for Cities-in-Schools with a visit to I.S. 22. Located near devastated sections of the South Bronx, this school also was featured in Mayor Koch's re-election campaign, highlighting neighborhood involvement in school reform as a political issue.

teeism dropped. Program people looked forward to showing further indications of personal self-improvement and a restoration of social ethic among these youths. (See Report 3, *Program Impact 1978–79* and especially the table reproduced here as Table 6.)

But in Atlanta and Manhattan the quality of record keeping remained low. The CIS program was not considered a success there, at least not by the prescribed evaluation standards. In Atlanta data flow from district computers became sporadic, then stopped altogether for more than a year. The CIS city director there, David Lewis, was not greatly disturbed by this breakdown, feeling that AIR should get other evidence of program effectiveness. Much later he told interviewer Naomi Richmond "I think some of the AIR staff were sensitive to the needs of the people in the program, but at the same time they didn't have time to look at everything. They had certain things to look for. . . . They knew what they were looking for and really didn't take time to look at the kinds of things I am talking about" (p. 3, Richmond file). Although he commended early evaluation efforts for pointing out needs for additional staff training and other organizational shortcomings, Lewis felt the original AIR evaluation design was simplistic and its operation too rigid to accommodate what AIR fieldworkers began to see for themselves.

The AIR staff reacted to such statements with exasperation. Murray once said.

Intimations that the CIS staff had these subtle indicators that we failed to examine are just plain wrong. From the first field trip, we urged CIS staff to describe the effects they saw as results of CIS, no matter how hard to measure. It would be our job to do justice to them. As it turned out, the indicators they came up with were behavioral ones that were incorporated into the data collection. I would challenge any member of CIS to name an effect that (1) would be a significant indication of success, (2) occurred among a significant number of CIS students, and (3) would not show up on our data collection instruments. (Personal communication to me upon reading draft of my NIE report, 1981.)

More will be said later about the validity of the AIR findings. But here it is noted again that the data gathering did not go smoothly in Atlanta, with strained relations among district, program, and evaluation groups.

In New York City administrative disagreements divided CIS efforts into separate enclaves. Formal records did not yield evidence of programmatic commitment, let alone evidence of aid to some of the city's estranged and distraught youth.

In all three cities the evaluators had personal knowledge that a large number of CIS people were vigorously at work with youngsters and that most stakeholders remained confident that CIS caseworkers were getting at the heart of juvenile problems. But only in Indianapolis in 1978–79 was there more than a minimal return of formal data. According to Murray, "Sample attrition killed us."

Actually there were several "killing" problems. During September and October 1979 (to begin the third year of the evaluation contract) Indianapolis teachers were on strike. CIS operations at all sites were undercut by delays in funding assurance. The statistical gains at Arsenal Tech were not repeated—in fact, it appeared some ground was lost. In New York City no progress was apparent to the outsiders. But some CIS eyes saw differently. In Atlanta David Lewis stated in his quarterly report: "The first quarter of this year was very productive. . . . Social Service statistics reflect an increase in home visits and staff was better able to deliver medical services to the youth . . .and their families" (p. 1). Lewis spoke further of intensive health screening, eleven field trips, and much participation of CIS youth in community activities. AIR evaluators did not challenge such inventories of activities, but from AIR data Smith High School showed no payoff in attendance, achievement, or lawfulness. When Smith High CIS Director Jimmy Hardy protested that success could be observed in terms of social services delivered on an individual basis, Murray asked him to identify a groups of youngsters most effectively turned around. Hardy named 18. Murray's intensive review of their records persuaded him that only in a few instances was individual success observable and enduring. He concluded that, on the whole, impact had to be judged negligible. Murray was satisfied that *however weak the evaluation assessment might be, there was no systematic improvement in these urban youth attributable to the Cities-in-Schools services.* He was certain there was no substantial Type II error, i.e., there was no substantial impact that AIR assessments failed to recognize. In the *Final Report* Murray provided little documentation of this lack of impact, but provided a careful review of the obstacles to impact.

A retrospective look at the calendar of the three-year evaluation study is detailed in Table 1. Events that might have had an important effect on the evaluation are also shown. In Figure 7 is the

AIR *proposed* schedule of activities. A comparison between these indicators of what was to have been done and what was done shows substantial similarity, but with these differences apparent:

1. considerable evaluator time was spent in meetings (confronting the contentiousness of a passionate and political enterprise)—less time than intended was spent on data processing;

2. the original plan underestimated the time that would actually be devoted to preparation of formal and informal reports;

3. the stakeholder groups required not only anticipated time to assist in design but also major blocks of time to review intermediate findings; and

4. the burden of writing such a difficult report, plus the stakeholder reviews of the final report, added an additional nine months to the study.

These differences will be examined further in the following section on personnel assignments for the evaluation study.

### Staffing

The AIR evaluation staffing plans called for a senior researcher (Charles Murray) to oversee the work of one Washington-based associate for each of the three cities, plus a data gatherer stationed at each site. Internally, senior personnel would advise and various specialists would assist. At each site the districts would employ additional data gatherers. The principal AIR associates and Murray himself would do a large share of the analysis and report writing, as well as carry the principal administrative liaison responsibilities. Murray preferred doing most of the quantitative work himself, once data storage was arranged.

*If in the end it is to be concluded that the evaluation work failed to aid the reform effort, or even was a deterrent to it—the background question of this book—it should be useful to consider how the evaluation time was spent.* If the evaluation project were understaffed, then unexpected and even unintended demands might be placed on CIS personnel. For example, the youthworkers might be asked to keep records they were unable to keep. What constitutes success might be treated less compromisingly. AIR personnel resources and obligations will be considered in detail in this section.

On the final page of his *Evaluation Design* Charles Murray presented a projected use of personnel by tasks, numbering 31 tasks to

Table 5. AIR-estimated Full-Time Equivalent Personnel
for Evaluation Tasks

|  | Staffing Levels | | |
|---|---|---|---|
|  | Senior Researchers | Project Associates | Research Assistants |
| Administrative liaison | 0.2 | 0.0 | 0.0 |
| Desk work, planning, development | 0.2 | 0.2 | 0.1 |
| Fieldwork, interviews, follow-up | 0.2 | 0.5 | 2.2 |
| Desk work, analysis | 0.1 | 0.2 | 0.4 |
| Desk work, reports | 0.5 | 0.3 | 0.1 |
| Total | 1.2 FTE | 1.2 FTE | 2.8 FTE |

be completed by senior staff, project associates, and research assistants. In Table 5 is a summary of Murray's estimates, grouped into task categories.

From the totals above we can conclude that this was a project for (the equivalent of) one senior researcher with a full-time associate and three full-time research assistants. It was presumed from the beginning that many people actually would work part-time and that there would be some attrition. The fieldwork would be a costly item. Report writing would be the most time-consuming responsibility of the senior researcher.

As indicated earlier, senior researchers Robert Krug and Jane Schubert at first expected to share considerably in the governance of the study, but they transferred to the Palo Alto AIR office soon after the project began. Senior researcher Victor Rouse made several key contributions early but was little involved later. Senior researcher Janice Redish supplied documentation for early conceptualizations of the social situation and the decision responsibility of public officials, but she was drawn to other work before the study was a year old.

Charles Murray was the only research person who stayed with the project from beginning to end. Blair Bourque was with the project from the end of the design phase through to termination in 1981, serving as Murray's principal associate for the last two years. An experienced associate, she took responsibility for work at the Indianapolis site. Less experienced associates, particularly Saundra Murray and Rigney Hill, were assigned to cover Atlanta and New York City. Hill probably spent as much time as anyone helping Murray think through the operational and liaison problems. It was not "career work" for her though, so she left AIR to become an urban hospital administrator. According to the CIS Atlanta view, Saundra Murray (no relation to Charles) was the fourth successive associate in Atlanta. Before the project was completed, she was promoted to a key responsibility for the AIR evaluation of PUSH/Excel. Dian Overby succeeded her. Another research associate, Susan Mileff, came along to assist with the final report. Such staffing changes unfortunately are not unusual in program evaluation work. They clearly have an effect, probably contributing to a greater mechanization, to a less deliberative approach to the research.

Except during monthly internal progress reviews (always by Paul Schwarz, sometimes with Victor Rouse attending) Murray seldom discussed—other than off-handedly—the CIS evaluation with other AIR researchers. Frequently, however, he reviewed details of all kinds with Norman Gold of NIE and had occasional conversations with his Technical Review Panel. Helen Branch of the Atlanta Public Schools and Elizabeth Baltz of CIS Indianapolis were often in communication with Murray. But it was very much a *one-researcher study.* Usually Charles Murray worked alone. Numerous author names appear on covers of reports, but analytic sections of reports were written almost entirely by Murray

A most serious personnel problem and operational difficulty occurred when Murray discovered in the final year that a major portion of the data-storage programming was badly flawed. He fired the programmer and redid the storage himself.

All personnel were assigned part-time. Murray, for example, was never officially more than half-time on CIS evaluation. Over the three-and-one-half-year contract period only about one-third of his salary was paid from this account. As is apparent in Table 6, he and others were heavily involved in work other than CIS. In the first ten months Murray was finishing a study called the Standards and Goals Project. In the second year he was involved in a controversy over interpretation of his UDIS Study.[3] At the same time he was be-

---

3. UDIS = Unified Delinquency Intervention Services (Chicago based).

Table 6. Full-Time-Equivalent Persons Assigned (for pay record purpose)
to the CIS Evaluation Study

Half-year periods beginning:

|                              | Oct. 77 | Apr. 78 | Oct. 78 | Apr. 79 | Oct. 79 | Apr. 80 | Oct. 80 |
|------------------------------|---------|---------|---------|---------|---------|---------|---------|
| Senior researchers           | 0.8     | 0.5     | 0.5     | 0.4     | 0.1     | 0.3     | 0.2     |
| Project associates           | 1.2     | 1.5     | 1.8     | 1.3     | 1.1     | 0.5     | 0.1     |
| Research assistants (data collection) | 0.1 | 1.1 | 1.0 | 1.7 | 1.7 | 0.5 | 0.7 |
| Data collector[4] (on site)  | —       | 1.25    | 2.5     | 2.5     | 2.5     | 1.25    | —       |

set with family problems. During the final year he and Saundra
Murray were heavily involved in beginning the evaluation of Jesse
Jackson's PUSH-to-Excellence project.

Disbursements of salary and wages often do not accurately indicate time spent on a research project. Still, it may be useful to see
how personnel salary and wages were charged at various stages of
this evaluation project.

The second year appears busiest by this record, but Charles
Murray explained that fast-rising costs caused project funds to be
consumed too early. Thus some large workloads during the last 18
months were charged to accounts other than Cities-in-Schools.

According to these salary disbursement records from AIR, even
at the busiest times this evaluation project did not employ a large
staff. Hypothetically, in a typical week one would find a senior researcher working slightly less than two and one-half days on the
study, backed up by three half-time research associates and three
half-time data collectors. Also (not shown in the table) there were
file managers, computer people, and secretaries who together ac-
counted for about the same total working time as the professional
researchers.[5]

---

4. This line did not appear on the "hours charged" summary provided
by AIR. Charles Murray indicated the on-site data collectors had been inad-
vertently excluded, and provided this data line.

5. According to Norman Gold, "The study was tightly budgeted, as is

Table 7. Estimated FTE Personnel Needed and Actual FTE Persons Paid

|                     | Needed | Paid |
|---------------------|--------|------|
| Senior researchers  | 1.2    | 0.5  |
| Project associates  | 1.2    | 1.2  |
| Research assistants | 2.8    | 1.1  |

As shown in Table 7, the research time charged to the evaluation project account was considerably less than the design estimates.[6] (Table 7 shows sums from the two previous tables.) Part of the reason, of course, was the fact that not nearly as many data were collected as expected. But it was not apparent from other observations that qualified colleagues were available to step into positions of responsibility had a need for them been recognized.

When asked to scale the productive contributions of individual staff members, Murray reluctantly allowed that he perhaps could accept credit for 40 percent of it. He credited Blair Bourque and Rigney Hill with another 25 percent and divided the remaining 35 percent into small increments among at least seven others. This was taken to mean that Murray himself also saw the evaluation of Cities-in-Schools as largely a one-researcher project.

Concerned about an inference the metaevaluator might be drawing, i.e., that the evaluation study team should have done more work for the size of the funding, Charles Murray wrote a personal letter saying:

I know it sounds idiotic to anyone not in the business, but the fact is that, even with a $730,000 project (or whatever it was), we had to scrimp on charges. Thus, I was originally slated to charge 75% of my time, as I remember, for three years. In actuality, I charged 2388 hours over 41 months, or 37.0%—almost exactly half of the intended charges. Why so little? Because we couldn't afford to charge more. Running extensive interview and archival data collection at multiple sites away from the central office is exceedingly expensive . . .

---

the NIE custom." It appeared Gold expected for this funding level more expert evaluation personnel working more time at the sites than was the case (private communication to me, February 1982).

6. The budget period was three years. For comparability the actual employment (over three and a half years) was increased by a factor of 3.5/3.0 to indicate employment as if it had occurred within those three years.

My actual hours? Take 11/79 through 3/80 as an example, the six months when I was writing the impact report. I charged 110 hours, or 11.6% of my time. You know my style, and that the report is my work. You also have an idea of the rate at which I do my analyses and writing—deliberate, to put it charitably. Overall, I must have put in at least 80 full days—at about ten hours each—during that six month period, and I bet a lot more. Yet the time charges suggest that I knocked out the analyses *and* the rough and smooth drafts in an aggregate of less than 15 days. (April 1982.)[7]

My intent here was not a technical review of the AIR payroll. (That was neither within my competence nor my assignment.) The amount of work actually done seemed to me to exceed the work anticipated in the Proposal narrative. Among other things I wanted to see if the actual endeavors allowed Charles Murray time to examine the CIS processes, political circumstances, and evolving perceptions of youth need. He did spend time this way, musing at length as to how to respond to CIS enterprises he had not foreseen. Ultimately, he returned to thinking of CIS as he had in the Proposal: a national demonstration project, an experimental program, a potential cause-and-effect relationship needing documentation.

Many observations confirm Murray's claim that the team worked hard. Yet the size and quality of the data collection were much less than anticipated. Some of the shortcomings in data collection were beyond Murray's control. But did he use his personnel budget as wisely as he could have, especially in maintaining expectation of studying the regression of attendance, achievement, and delinquency on program characteristics? By one view within the Technical Review Panel, what he purchased was what the evaluation study needed. Accordingly there was no need for redesign of data gathering, even when the intended treatments and testing were clearly not occurring. By another view, Murray should have redirected attention more quickly and more thoroughly to the reasons why the intended program was not occurring and to what was in fact occurring in the "real-world" diffusion of CIS services. Or should he have proposed postponement of evaluation work until the program activity was stabilized in the way his design required? He did so propose but such an alternative was contrary to political and contractual realities. He was committed to the personnel workload indicated more or less in the proposal. Options were few and limited.

---

7. Paul Schwarz confirmed that "in the later stages, huge amounts of uncompensated time were spent, notably by Charles."

## Data Collection and Feedback

Of the evaluation study's several purposes, the major one was to test[8] the *general idea* of aid to "high risk" youth (and their families) through integrated social services operating in and out of the schools.[9] Educational researchers usually prefer designing experiments to test general ideas. As with almost all evaluations of federal demonstration projects the "treatment" was not under researcher control. Assignments could not be randomized. A few "comparison groups" available were not strictly comparable, but possibly useful. A correlational analysis statistically linking outcome variables to treatment variables was seen as the strongest design AIR could use to produce generalizable knowledge about the impact of social services integration efforts.[10]

Accordingly, the evaluation plan directed data collection toward the effects on youth, with attention as needed to services integration and caseworker activity. Program people, stakeholders, and evaluation people decided early that attendance, academic achievement (particularly in reading), and trouble with the police would serve as the measurable indicators of program impact. Greater rehabilitation impact was desired, and expected. The measured variables were intermediate, incremental goals rather than ultimate. By consensus they were seen as necessary steps for full success and positive correlates with other forms of impact.[11]

Partly to minimize the redundancy of testing and record keep-

---

8. For this present review of AIR evaluation work the raw data files were not examined. Authenticating data presentations or generating alternative interpretations of those data were not seen as purposes deserving that much probing.

9. The CIS people, however, did not envision the idea of a *general* test of services integration and casework in schools. They saw CIS not as representative of a class of social treatments but as a fixed particular. Good results might help promote CIS installation elsewhere.

10. One important indication of Charles Murray's thinking about what program evaluation should be was his commitment to three preliminary evaluation report names: Program Description, Program Process, and Program Impact. That separation meant less emphasis on history, economics, program development, operations problems, and policy issues. This was to be an analytic rather than a holistic study, detailing the variables under the three titles.

11. At the outset Charles Murray appeared confident that these mini-

ing and partly because circumstances varied at the different sites, there was no uniform (across sites) measurement of these outcome variables. District records on attendance and achievement would be used. (Delivery was "assured" by special contract between NIE and the districts.) Regular achievement testing would be augmented as necessary but would be performed by the schools rather than by evaluators. CIS caseworkers would keep case records. AIR interviewers would obtain police records and conduct interviews to record process variables and background conditions, as well as to back up the measurement of impact.

Of course, it would require considerable work by the evaluators to become thoroughly acquainted with the program. First acquaintance was shared with insiders and outsiders through the publication of the evaluation project's first report, *Program Description*: "Information was gathered by personal observation, interviews, and written responses from the managers of the projects, combined with less formal exposure to watching classes, sitting in on counseling sessions, or going along to a basketball practice, a pizza party, or a neighborhood cleanup" (p. iii, Report 1).

It was apparent to the evaluators at that early time that program treatment would vary from site to site and that treatment would continue to evolve. The more commonly publicized "family structure" (40 students with four caseworkers) was already more associated with Arsenal Tech in Indianapolis, Julia Richman in New York, and two public high schools in Atlanta.[12]

The first round of process data feedback made the evaluation team uneasy. It would be difficult to make sense of the design (its finishing touches were still being put in place) with such an elusive treatment. The doubts increased during data gathering that following fall (1978): ". . . it became apparent that in many respects we were evaluating a different program from the one we had started to examine in the spring of 1978. Selection criteria, staffing, program-

---

mal goals would be achieved. He indicated that his problem would be diagnostic, i.e., identifying why CIS worked for some youngsters and not for others.

12. Among the program data reported by AIR at that time: that federal funding to CIS for FY78 was set at $2,300,000; that CIS was presently (February 1978) serving 2,800 students, with 34 participating social service agencies, including the school districts and other government offices (p. 5, Report 1).

matic emphases, administrative structure—all had changed, sometimes radically, over the summer" (p. 4, Report 2). Which students were actually enrolled in the program, which had dropped out, and which were "camp followers" was far more important to the evaluators than to the CIS staff. Financial support for the CIS work could be obtained from additional sources by adding new goals or changing admission criteria. Resources could be optimized by letting program boundaries remain vague. The evaluators found misrepresentations as to what was being done, who was doing it, and for what agency. Murray pointed out that gain measurements would appear small if students with lesser needs, i.e., with lesser deficits in the criterion dimensions, were allowed to be counted. He counseled CIS directors that discrepancies between CIS rhetoric and action, and even inconsistencies among sites, would ultimately work against the program.

One problem for Murray was the absence of a strong central command within CIS. More expansionist than consolidator, Milliken was busy at the time kindling new support and refueling old. Though serving as Indianapolis city director, Oostdyk was also busy promoting new ventures. Both encouraged and endorsed the management at the several sites, but neither provided procedural focus to program administrators. The two of them were dismayed but not surprised by Murray's feedback. They made efforts to change some things but did not really redirect their attentions to the "demonstration" going on in Atlanta, Indianapolis, and New York City. Murray felt forced to work on organizational details with separate administrators at each site.

One of the key discrepancies the evaluators observed was in "services integration." In official CIS statements the restructuring of social services was a necessary step toward better assistance without increased costs: "Cities-in-Schools operates on the premise that our society is presently investing sufficient resources to meet the needs of its youth. The reason we are not realizing the return on our investments centers on the method by which resources and services are delivered" (quoted on p. 6, Report 2).

But the evaluators observed little "services integration" success and, as time went on, little effort on the part of CIS to compromise with the agencies' definitions of service. At an August meeting with CIS directors, the evaluators asked for rating of program goals. This "services integration" goal fell well below "assisting youth personal growth" and about the same as "improving student performance" and "institutionalizing the CIS approach." After thorough analysis of caseworker training and experience, Murray and his coauthors noted:

> . . . The constraints on the money (e.g., for employing CETA workers) and CIS's dependence on others (e.g., the agencies deciding who to second to the program) have often put CIS in the position of either taking the people it could get or else backing down on its commitments to mount a program of a given size in a given school. CIS has chosen to take what it could get.
>
> This has been palatable to CIS in part because, despite its rhetoric, some senior officials in CIS have exhibited skepticism about the role of professional skills. (P. 74, Report 2.)

Thus, regarding one major promise, Cities-in-Schools efforts were seen to be far off the track.

The evaluators made only a quiet fuss. The "services integration" issue was placed in the middle of the evaluation report on process and introduced with a disingenuous statement of rating data that said, "The service integration goal remains a high priority. According to the responses of senior CIS staff, it is second only to the fundamental service goal of assisting the students' personal growth" (p. 72, Report 2).

Drawing little attention to the priority of "services integration" may have helped AIR maintain working relationships with the program. It may have seemed to Murray that the issue was more ideological than practical. The fact was that CETA program temporary employees were available as caseworkers, and few regular social service agency people—firemen or social workers—were available. The fact that CIS "families" then had little new contact with the cities' resources was regrettable—but somehow not a part of the evaluators' purview.

Had the evaluation design been "emergent" or "progressively focussed" (as recommended by Parlett and Hamilton, 1972) rather than pre-specified, and had service to stakeholders been optimized, this issue might have been developed for consideration of stakeholder groups. Local stakeholders probably would have appreciated a chance to react to the implications of these personnel arrangements. Some of these issues were developed in AIR's *Final Report* but not as on-going dialogue with stakeholders.

When Report 2 was circulated the following spring, CIS directors objected to Murray's mild criticisms.[13] They declared the services integration goal was no longer critical. The "supportive education" role for CETA-provided caseworkers was the new top priority. At the time of writing that report Murray had remembered several members of the Technical Review Panel, meeting in California the previous August (1978), strongly protesting the change in CIS rationale. It was a difficult bind for the evaluators. Was services integration a key goal or not?

But even more troubling were the 1977–78 enrollment data Murray studied. He found large numbers of students to have only an educational problem or a poverty problem; for them the Cities-in-Schools arrangements seemed an "over-reaction." As to need for better management at the sites, CIS program people agreed with the criticism of Report 2. (Later some argued that those rationale, enrollment, and management problems were already quite apparent and that the evaluation study merely reinforced awarenesses.)

Here, then, was another emergent issue: *admission criteria.* Murray recognized it in terms of jeopardy to the statistical analysis but not as one of considerable educational significance. It is common for special purpose (categorical) programs such as courses for gifted youngsters, when they are good, to attract students other than those for whom the programs were originally intended. Educators and parents want lots of youngsters to have this new opportunity. The more heterogeneous student group causes the teaching to change, dissipating or even contradicting the original purpose.

Here AIR was facing an important general issue about special opportunity programs, important for institutionalizing Cities-in-Schools elsewhere in the world. It could have been examined in terms of experience in other categorical programs. Unfortunately, this CIS evaluation design more or less forced the admissions problem to be treated as a technical problem.

With these problems at hand, their second year in the schools (1978–79) the evaluators became engaged in a much more formative evaluation effort than anticipated. They frequently advocated strict maintenance of the original demonstration plan as distinct from school-by-school adaptation to local needs and conditions. This

---

13. Murray provided space to CIS in the appendices of Report 2 for rebuttal.

advocacy and formative collaboration called for expenditures of time and energy well beyond budgetary allocations.

Norman Gold had once suggested that CIS stakeholders could expect feedback every 180 days "concerning program implementation, as well as progress on appropriate impact measures" (p. 12, Gold file). Of course different stakeholder groups would be more directly informed than others. Feedback on problems of program development was not provided to funding agency stakeholders at all. No alteration in funding was made, or anticipated, as a result of early evaluation work. (This is not meant to suggest it should have been. Had program support been contingent on early feedback, it is likely that both program and evaluation would have been greatly debilitated.) It was apparent that the initial definitions of stakeholder evaluation left much unsaid as to what information should be released to which stakeholders. The presumption usually was maintained that still-to-be-gotten impact data would be most important.

## Impact Data

Collection of impact data by AIR and the districts began during the spring of 1978 and continued through spring 1980. The *Impact Report* (Report 3) was written during that last winter and circulated in draft form (as was the practice) throughout the spring and even into the summer.

The language of impact used by AIR evaluators continued to move attention toward earlier intermediate objectives, spoken of as "investment behaviors" and even "preinvestment behaviors." Indicators of those behaviors are listed in Table 8, a gross summary of impact taken from Report 3.

The *Impact Report* section on conclusions included the following paragraphs:

The differences among the sites are so great that they affect all of the conclusions. It is essential to separate out statements about CIS-the-concept from CIS as it exists at the sites we observed.

If the only site we observed had been Tech at Indianapolis, the overall assessment would be quite positive and optimistic. This is in spite of the fact that, as the process report made clear, major problems of implementation remain in Indianapolis. The program at Tech is far from being as well structured, staffed, and administered as it could be. Further, the problems that exist are ones that impede impact on the student. Yet, even while operating at a relatively low level of efficiency, the program is yielding a pattern of

Table 8. AIR Gross Summary of the Impact of CIS

| Outcome | Smith | Carver | Tech | Julia Richman |
|---|---|---|---|---|
| | | (NA: Not Available) | | |
| 1. Increased understanding of options and requirements | – | NA | + | NA |
| 2. Increased sense of control over the future | NA | NA | + | + |
| 3. Stricter standards of personal behavior | – | ± | + | – |
| 4. Increased voluntary learning | ± | ± | ± | + |
| 5. Increased attention and effort in the classroom | – | ± | + | – |
| 6. Reduced voluntary absences, cuts | – | – | ± | – |
| 7. Increased success in interpersonal relations | ± | + | + | – |
| 8. Increased success in learning situations | + | ± | + | ± |
| 9. Acquisition of basic reading skills | + | NA | + | NA |
| 10. Reduced official delinquency | + | + | ± | NA |
| 11. Higher attendance | – | – | + | ± |
| 12. Higher grades | ± | ± | ± | ± |

Source: *The National Evaluation of the Cities-in-Schools Program. Report No. 3: Program Impact* (1978–79), p. 83.

positive results. Putting together all that we have found to date, CIS at Tech can legitimately argue that it has important, positive impact on the educational and social development of a substantial number of students who enter the program.

. . .

When Atlanta and New York are brought into the picture, the conclusions get fuzzier. On many of the indicators where Tech showed positive results, the other sites showed deterioration.

These conclusions and the entries of the summary table above were backed up with attendance records, arrest figures, and test scores. Many data were missing, particularly from the Atlanta public schools.

In Atlanta data processing responsibility had been reassigned by the superintendent from the central finance office to the research division. Apparently in protest, a number of technical people quit their jobs. Well more than a year went by without provision of key impact data. Murray sought alternative data sources without success. Details of that situation are indicated in the following *interview excerpt*:

On May 6, 1982, I went to the Research and Evaluation Division of the Atlanta Public Schools. I talked with Jarvis Barnes, the Assistant Superintendent, with Research Associate Myrtice Taylor and Research Assistants Andrew Plankenhorn and Richard Horton.[14]

Stake: (after personal exchange) Let me start with the hardest question. Why was information flow limited between APS and AIR?

Barnes: Things were fluid then. There were changes in the "main players": program staff, data processors, etc. Data processing responsibilities were moved in 1979 from Finance to Research. People left. We had difficulty supplying information to the whole system.

Taylor: This office had difficulty staying in touch with the evaluation group. Norm Gold and Charles Murray insisted on Helen Branch remaining as the data liaison person even though she had transferred to the Area III office in "instruction."

Plankenhorn: Charlie had to contend with the parameters. The process of designing the evaluation was not ours. When we tried to provide these data we had problems.

Barnes: We had our share of charges. We have been in a period of "catch-up"—just "staying alive." There has been difficulty supplying information for the whole school system. But the AIR evaluation study was especially difficult. Many students there, for example, did not have ID numbers. (pause) Actually, we were never very much involved. Charlie more or less set up his own process. It was not our job.

Taylor: These are some of the problems we ran into. Those (CIS) folks were mighty independent even though they were practically part of the system. Our regulations say that in order to receive assistance poor students must be registered in a certain way to be assigned an ID number.

---

14. After reading these excerpts Taylor wrote, "The write-up is not truly representative of what we thought we said . . . basically all that went wrong with the evaluation stemmed from mechanical and personnel problems within the Research and Evaluation Division." (Some of the remainder of the interview appears on p. 94).

Table 9. Number of Days Students Were Absent

|  | 7th | 8th | 9th | 10th |
|---|---|---|---|---|
|  | (1st year CIS) | | (2nd year CIS) | |
| 1976–77 CIS freshmen | 23.0 | 27.1 | 43.8 | 67.6 |
| n | 34 | 34 | 34 | 36 |
| 1977–78 CIS freshmen | 26.5 | 29.3 | 46.1 | 50.4 |
| n | 42 | 43 | 47 | 26 |
| 1978–79 CIS freshmen | —* | —* | 50.1 | |
| n | | | 78 | |

*Data are being provided by the APS but had not arrived as of this writing.

Source: *The National Evaluation of the Cities-in-Schools Program. Report No. 3: Program Impact* (1980), p. 65.

Well, there were kids who would walk in and say, "I want to come." That was fine when he was there. A year later they would say, "Hey, what was his attendance?" We didn't know who or what we had.

Stake: Would these have been students who dropped out or people who had just moved into town?

Barnes: Both. Some operators of the program felt that they had their own things to do, separate and apart from the school system. Any program that operates separately from the school environment is going to tumble sooner or later and cause friction in the District. Finally, the Board spelled out the District's responsibility. That was when things began to get straightened out.

Plankenhorn: We were disappointed. The first year, working with the California Achievement Test, we only had about 20% of students with pre and post scores. . . .

Even after "things got straightened out," Charles Murray did not get the Atlanta data base he needed.

The principal indicators of incremental success were, as identified earlier, school achievement, attendance, and avoidance of trouble with the police. At Arsenal Tech *reading gains* from fall to spring were shown to be substantial but problematic. Attendance was shown in tables such as Table 9. Changes—or lack of change— in the probability of arrest were summarized for schools as shown in Table 10.

Again, these results were not presented for all years, and often only for small numbers of students; the data thus were unsuitable for use in the intended statistical analyses. Results for the third

Table 10. Changes in Arrest and Probability of Rearrest

| | n | Total Arrests Year Prior | Total Arrests, Year After Entering | Change |
|---|---|---|---|---|
| Smith | 35 | 15 | 21 | +40% |
| Carver | 21 | 6 | 1 | −83% |
| Tech | 104 | 11 | 24 | +118% |

| | Smith | | Tech | |
|---|---|---|---|---|
| Probability of re-arrest after . . . | Pre-CIS | During CIS | Pre-CIS | During CIS |
| 1 prior arrest | 55% | 42% | 30% | 37% |
| 2 prior arrests | 55% | 56% | 38% | 42% |
| 3 prior arrests | 83% | 17% | 40% | 44% |
| 4 prior arrests | 60% | 100% | | |
| 5 prior arrests | 100% | 67% | | |
| 6 prior arrests | 60% | 100% | | |

Source: *The National Evaluation of the Cities-in-Schools Program. Report No. 3: Program Impact* (1978–79), p. 63.

year were promised stakeholders in a September (1980) report. Charles Murray drafted and circulated the *Final Report* about then but provided only the most general summary statements about third-year impact. That impact had not improved in Atlanta and New York City and had fallen back in Indianapolis, probably partly because a teacher strike there delayed school opening for two months and funding delays brought further disruption.

Murray had designed an elaborate study of impact indicators, but he failed to obtain the data for a proper analysis. The data he did obtain did not indicate a substantial improvement in attendance and achievement, or a reduction of unlawful behavior. As will be told in the section on the *Final Report*, Murray probed the better data sources at length, hoping to find previously undiscovered positive results. This hunt too was largely unsuccessful.

## NIE Monitoring

The technical monitoring of the AIR contract went along in a routine and satisfactory manner. Recalling the history of AIR evaluation of CIS, NIE's Norman Gold told a gathering of "policy board stakeholders" in Indianapolis:

> We took the program you brought us and developed an evaluation model that was systematic and disciplined. Not scientific. We couldn't do that in your schools system and in your community. We know when that is tried, it is notoriously disruptive and doesn't tell you any more. Loud and clear, we heard the need for controls—and we said we don't think they are worth it.
>
> This evaluation report will be aimed at the investment of the students, what they say about their willingness to invest, how they perceive the school, how they perceive what they are doing in classes. It is enormously important to us, and to you. It's enormously important to everyone in this room that, in fact, those students were saying that they are trying harder, they are doing better, they are reading more, they are starting to invest in their education. (P. 8, Transcript, 30 June 1980.)

Gold's monitoring was personal and intense. Gold and Murray got along well, saw each other socially as well as on business. Norman was proprietorial about the evaluation study, frequently using the pronoun "we" to describe who was doing it. He urged—and exemplified—high ethical and professional standards.

He was proprietorial also about the stakeholder idea. From the podium at the the 1980 meeting of the Evaluation Research Society, Gold spoke of the importance of this opportunity to study the "stakeholder process." He twice took credit for creating the notion, relating it to capacity for program development and decision making.

Gold stressed a continuing working relationship between evaluators and decision makers to orient studies toward producing useful information. As examples of stakeholders he mentioned federal agency officials, local government people, service-providing agencies, consumers, and other evaluators and program developers.

He spoke against too passive a response by evaluators, charging them to judge the needs expressed by stakeholders in terms of the capacity of evaluators to serve those needs. In subsequent reflection about CIS, he claimed that AIR evaluation work had become part of local decision making. But he noted that officials (stakeholders) at the federal level felt they had no *decision responsibility* to be influenced by outcomes of the study. Gold said that in general the emphasis on stakeholders paid off in clarifying what to expect from the AIR study. "It makes it more responsive."

One person, and essentially only one person, represented the federal government in this evaluation study.[15] Others were not involved "developmentally" in learning what the evaluation team was learning about CIS work. Gold preferred to work pretty much by himself. And his office colleagues may have resisted opportunities to learn—Gold did occasionally pontificate. At the Indianapolis stakeholders' meeting cited above, Gold listened perplexedly to long and quarrelsome criticism of the AIR *Impact Report* by a dubious associate superintendent, then interceded:

> As I understand it, we are here because it is important for you to know if the Program is as good as the CIS people say it is. In Atlanta we said the program was not so good. There wasn't much [objection]. But when we say it is good here, there is a big [objection].
>
> What I want to make sure of, when we leave here, is that *you know* that this is a good evaluation; that you know it represents what we are capable of doing, the state of the art. It was paid by your public dollars, done by people who have spent years and years trying to figure how to do it right, not to leave a mess when through.
>
> I want to make sure we are not playing games. I want questions raised until there is no doubt left. We can make mistakes. I don't want us to walk away from this room uncertain. I want to be sure you are convinced this is a good study, that you can rely on it, as good as anything of its kind. (Transcript, Policy Board Meeting, 30 June 1980.)

At NIE during this period Gold held the title "Senior Research Associate for Evaluation." His task generally was to study and improve evaluation use strategies. In a 1978 reorganization he—along with a dozen or so other specialists in educational measurements and evaluation—became part of a division called "Testing, Assessment and Evaluation." They gave considerable emphasis to assessing the utility of evaluation studies and sought ways of manipulating factors that influence utility. The "stakeholder approach" was one such way. Others were "the national hearing process" and "the convening process."[16]

According to Gold, "When real evaluation studies are planned, people in this division take a pretty conventional approach. But

---

15. Gold and his NIE associates pointed out that it was standard federal practice to have only one person assigned to such a project, and then only as *part* of a full assignment.

16. NIE colleague Enid Herndon at this time was monitoring a "national hearing" of competency-based testing and Gold himself was getting the "convening process" tried out in the Washington, D.C. schools.

there is not a high expectation that those studies will be productive. I have been able to get some acceptance of the stakeholder approach because of its greater potential for use." Gold acknowledged that the stakeholder approach was likely to redirect attention to local contexts, perhaps requiring ethnographic data. Such redirection was not encouraged by his colleagues. Gold continued: "When *they* look for something important in evaluation they look for the believable, and that means tables and test scores. The rest is too fluffy and floppy" (oral communication, 25 February 1982).

Jeffrey Schiller, the person in charge of the division, was, with reservation, supportive of the more political-and-process-oriented evaluation innovations Gold promoted. With CIS here, he felt the stakeholder notion had been too broadly construed. Schiller remained interested in whether or not the evaluation study accomplished its goals, but he showed little interest in findings about Cities-in-Schools.

Another NIE person interested in evaluation research methods was Charles Stalford, group leader for evaluation. He too had reservations, partly about the diminishing emphasis on test scores, but he assisted in the development of the stakeholder ideas. In a paper delivered to the annual meeting of the Evaluation Network (a sister organization to the Evaluation Research Society), he declared NIE interest in both quantitative and qualitative evaluation, especially to serve "prospective adopters" who need good descriptions of "process" to judge whether a program could be accommodated locally. Stalford also spoke of NIE concern for the issues of "fairness and justice" raised by Ernest House, declaring that the stakeholder approach used to evaluate Cities-in-Schools was responsive to those issues.

This is to say that there was an NIE interest in monitoring the AIR evaluation operation to see if it remained on track and produced findings. There was little interest in the substance of the findings, e.g., what are we learning about relieving the problems of urban youth. Elsewhere, in federal offices, Kathlyn Moses kept in touch but did not see herself as a disseminator of findings. The several federal funding agencies making up the CIS consortium showed no interest in the AIR-NIE effort, apparently feeling *coerced* into supporting CIS rather than, as one agency head put it, "other programs further developed conceptually and more worthy of support." Of course there continued to be interest in whether or not "the White

House" might become embarrassed by failure or enhanced by a sterling performance of CIS. Reporter Spencer Rich of the *Washington Post* telephoned NIE occasionally but published none of the AIR findings, intermediate or eventual.

All this was long before the "new federalism" of the Reagan administration. The National Institute of Education was always limited to a budget "already-spent," but was presumed all that time to be part of the long-term apparatus of federal support for education. The plight of the cities was not a popular cause, but expectations continued that massive support would ultimately come to rescue school and social service agencies and their clients. Social programs were troublesomely expensive, but the expectation was for more, not fewer, of them. And still, in 1978 and 1979, there was an almost complete absence of interest in the AIR effort to measure CIS efforts to demonstrate an alternative way to help those youth worse off. There essentially was no optimism in the federal establishment that something important would be learned.

No time-tested, meticulous, ideological monitoring of the substance of programs existed at NIE. NIE followed the lead of social science in its epistemological preference for scaled data as opposed to the kinds of case data used in law. That may be part of the reason educational research findings are too little used (see Schubert, 1980, p. 22). The rhetoric of federal support of educational research implies that NIE will learn from its research and be in a position to advise policy makers. That capacity was not apparent in this case.

Norman Gold did learn, and was meticulous and caring, but no other federal person was learning from the evaluation study. *It was supposed that anything worth knowing about CIS would be contained in formal reports—even though it is common practice to rely heavily on personal contacts in preparing briefings for policy makers.* AIR reports greatly under-reported the CIS story that Murray and Gold knew. Gold made occasional initiatives to persuade and inform, but down corridors and across buildings throughout the federal community CIS remained no more than a political incident. It was not presumed Gold had something important to say. A large part of $800,000 was spent to educate Norman Gold, with little expectation he would then teach others. Gold said: "When I finished this study, I was the loneliest man in the world. Carter was gone. Califano was gone. They were all gone. But I guess the intrinsic interest of the federal government never was there. It makes me think I have even more responsibility to get the stakeholder concept better known" (oral communication, 26 February 1982).

When we think of the role of the federal government we sometimes are inclined to think of impersonal action and reaction. In this instance at least, it was as imbued with "personalism" as any of CIS's own youthwork episodes.

### Advice from the Technical Review Panel

This evaluation study brought together two grand corporations, .the U.S. government and the American Institutes for Research. Yet, as represented in idea and deed by Charles Murray and Norman Gold, the work was highly personal and particularistic.[17] One intended counterbalance to such "personalism" was the conventional wisdom of researchers, here to be drawn from the Evaluation Research Society in the form of a Technical Review Panel. As introduced earlier (in Chapter Two) the Technical Review Panel was to provide advice—yes, perhaps—but principally to assure that the evaluation strategy was sound.

Some further "early history" may be of value. The Christmas Eve (1977) letter of invitation from ERS President, Robert Perloff, set the brief:

Our task, as an evaluation research review technical panel, will be twofold. First, to advise and consult with AIR on their evaluation design, concerning which over the next three years we will have several meetings and conferences. Next, it is hoped that we will be able to develop procedures and examine methodologies efficacious for conducting interactive field-based evaluations that might be of some value heuristically to the funding agency, the NIE, to methodologists in general, and to evaluation researchers in particular.

Six panel members (including myself) joined three AIR researchers and Gold for a get-acquainted drink at the Hilton in downtown Indianapolis late on a cold 19th of January, 1978. Discussions began that night. The next day was devoted to a visit to Arsenal Tech.

---

17. This is not to say the CIS evaluation study was more "personal" than other evaluation research at the time, whether qualitative or quantitative in approach. It is not to say the work was casual or irrational. It is merely to say that the activity and operation of the project repeatedly reflected the talents and persuasions of the persons in charge and were not impersonal as a literal reading of the contract, plans, and reports imply.

There we panelists met CIS program people, heard an optimistic ré-
sumé by CIS City Director Oostdyk and remarks by a proud host,
Ray Reed, the principal. The size of the program, the budget at Tech,
and the degree to which CIS students there were isolated from other
students were perhaps the outstanding impressions.

On the following day Murray, with inserts from Robert Krug
and Jane Schubert, outlined the evaluation situation, highlighted
materials distributed then or earlier, and solicited help in completing his already long list of impact variables. The discussions began.

Only small attention was given to measurement per se, that
best pursued by Malcolm Klein regarding indicators of youth involvement with the juvenile justice system and indicators of social
services integration. Ward Edwards expressed concern about the
crude representation of project goals and priorities. Eugene Webb
wanted to find ways of doing mini-experiments within the overall
plan. I pushed for greater commitment to collecting "process data,"
particularly observations of teaching and counseling. Gene Glass
indicated dismay over the lack of evaluator desire to record CIS
"paternalism" and "self-righteousness." Here, and at subsequent
panel meetings, in various ways and to varying degrees, we panelists voiced indignation, enlisted Murray's attention to separate
points of view, argued vigorously with whomever appeared not persuaded, made suggestions, and genuinely enjoyed ourselves. Chairman Perloff agreed with most of the suggestions, reminding everyone that there were many contradictions in the "advice" being
given. Votes were not taken. Unanimity was rare.

Panelist attention to the stakeholder dimension was minimal. It
seemed more important to find ways to apply the controls and measure the dependent variables to produce sound generalizations about
services delivery in the school setting. But already in that first January it was apparent that "coordinating services" was—to CIS people
there—not the treatment, not a pressing issue. Student eligibility
criteria remained unsettled—playing havoc with the definition of
the CIS "treatment groups." The diversity of definitions of "what
CIS is" was already getting in the way of the effort to generalize.

## Issues

At that first panel meeting observer Jennifer McCreadie of
CIRCE identified a number of issues, some implicit, some discussed.
Abstracted, these were:

1. Which students should get CIS full attention?
2. Is it okay to concentrate pedagogy on teaching reading skills?
3. Is it okay to ignore vocational education? (at a voc ed high school?)
4. What is happening to the school programs for non-CIS students?
5. Is the staff devoting sufficient time to the central tasks?
6. What is the effect of the program's "paternalism"?
7. Are there beneficiaries other than students?
8. Do agency staffers who volunteer for reassignment differ from "conscripts"?
9. Is there sufficient trust among the agencies?
10. What "costs" are there to ordinary city social services?

Evaluation design issues she noted were:

1. How to win better acceptance among program people.
2. How seriously to take program goal rhetoric.
3. How much to insist on arrangements to aid evaluation.
4. How to identify what caseworkers were doing for youth.
5. How much to attend to variants of program "pure form."
6. How much to invest in trying to produce strong generalization.

Panelist pessimism perhaps equaled program staff optimism. Charles Murray remained somewhere in between. He was going to be sure to record what seemed almost certain: the students' first "investment" on their way back. Still troubled by the emphasis on *impact*, I pressed further (in correspondence) for "probing the bejeebers out of the program rather than doing conceptual, generalizable basic research, . . . to find out what is good and bad about the program, not what is the principal cause of the principal effect" (letter dated 24 January 1978). In a hasty, cordial note, Murray responded:

I remain thoroughly uninterested in many of the process topics until I know whether many important behaviors are being changed among the kids. In particular, I want to get at *changes* in behavior of these kids. If Cities-in-Schools implements the concept reasonably well in a large enough number of cases for us to examine (i.e., does provide the level of personalism, accountability, and integration of services that they have taken as their objective) and their evaluation is not able to pick up any meaningful signs that this had an impact on the behavior, *that* will be, I think, a profoundly important finding. (Letter dated 9 February 1978.)

The discussions continued in New Orleans' Le Downtowner Du Vieux Carre in early April. Gene Glass was not there but David Wiley was. Those two had somewhat similar backgrounds, but Wiley picked up on matters of design strategy rather than substantive issues. Supported generally by Klein, Webb, Gold, and Perloff, as well as Wiley, the importance of strong designs, experimental or correlational, was pressed again upon a willing evaluation researcher.

In June Murray sent panelists the final version of the *Evaluation Design*, noting:

Three of your consensus recommendations are reflected in the text: that we explore the possibility of using service/no service as the basis for developing comparison groups; that we increase our emphasis on the "surround" of the school and the community; and that we reflect on how unlikely the four routes toward institutionalization actually are. . . .

Another issue, that we are getting too close to the program,[18] was not raised in the design. We did hear you clearly. (Letters dated 13 June 1978.)

Shortly thereafter the first data were coming in from the sites. Almost immediately (one thinks of Frank Skeffington in *The Last Hurrah*) Charles Murray knew he was in trouble: "Our findings were unbelievedly bleak. Judging from what we had been told by the caseworkers themselves, students had relatively few 'problems,' except that they were doing poorly in school. The incidence of 'service delivery' other than general counseling was very low. Few caseworkers had developed much knowledge about the family situation. And so on, through a litany of inadequacies" (p. 8, "Issues for the Technical Review Panel").

Intervention

Murray sketched a dozen pages of graphs and charts, such as that in Table 11, showing that the CIS students were not much different from the schools' other students and that the caseworkers did not have a consistency of language, intervention strategy, or philosophy.

At a 3–4 August meeting at Asilomar State Park near Monterey, California, Murray sought further advice from the Technical Review Panel. He indicated that if there was to be any chance of a successful evaluation study, he would have to go much further than he would like in insisting that CIS directors get their programs straightened out. "Did the panel agree?"

---

18. Seeing AIR's empathy for services integration and Murray's sympathy for a troubled CIS staff, we panelists talked at length about the dangers for cooption, "going native," and substituting formative evaluation for summative evaluation.

Table 11. Chart of Student/Staff Member Agreement on the CIS Program

| | Student/Staff Member Agreement (Sample = Eligibles) | | | | |
|---|---|---|---|---|---|
| | A<br>Both<br>agree<br>"yes" | B<br>CM says<br>yes, Stu-<br>dent no | C<br>CM says<br>no, stu-<br>dent yes | Both<br>agree<br>"no" | |
| Helped provide . . . | | | | | |
| Medical Care | 7 | 14 | 3 | 57 | +11 |
| Child care | 0 | 1 | 1 | 78 | 0 |
| Social Security | 0 | 2 | 1 | 76 | +1 |
| Welfare | 1 | 3 | 1 | 73 | +2 |
| Consumer problem | 0 | 1 | 1 | 77 | 0 |
| Legal help | 1 | 6 | 2 | 71 | +4 |
| Employment | 1 | 4 | 11 | 64 | -7 |
| Student ever . . . | | | | | |
| Hunted by police | 9 | 8 | 7 | 43 | +1 |
| Been taken to court | 9 | 4 | 1 | 54 | +3 |
| Been on probation | 3 | 5 | 1 | 61 | |

Source: Charles Murray, "Issues for the Technical Review Panel" (1981).

The panel discussed the matter for hours. I led the opposition, arguing that the program belonged to CIS, that evaluator demands impeded operations, and that the evaluators should evaluate the program they ran, not the one that the evaluators thought should be run. Eugene Webb took a somewhat similar stand. Malcolm Klein stood firm for intervention, arguing that *here* the research was more important than the service, that CIS and all urban communities had a chance to learn what services integration, "personalism," and a "holistic developmental" approach could do for estranged youth. Ward Edwards took a somewhat similar stand.

Victor Rouse, by then Murray's immediate superior at AIR, argued that evaluator intrusiveness is inevitable, that merely being on the scene does most of the damage, and that helping program people make difficult changes may help the program more than hurt it. Ward Edwards presented an elaborate plan for encouraging CIS staff to think out more systematically what they wanted to accomplish.[19]

19. Along the lines of Ward Edwards, Marcia Guttentag, and Kurt Snapper's "A Decision-Theoretic Approach to Evaluation Research."

Charles Murray took note of these several persuasions and departed, bound for the three sites to confront directors and stakeholders. *That* more or less ended panel advising on design strategy. Murray continued to keep the group informed. In April he and Gold flew to Los Angeles to talk things over with Klein, Edwards, and Perloff. Another eighteen months passed. Then panelists were brought together in Chicago for a final time to consider alternative presentations of the final report.[20] That meeting is covered in the next section.

### Discussion of *Final Report* Issues

In a small way it is social science which is on trial in this book. The federal government required the reform effort to be evaluated and imposed some of the conceptualization. A commercial research organization contracted to do the evaluation work and provided some of the conceptualization. But both of these, as pointed out by Ernest House (1977) and David Cohen (1983), draw heavily on the authority of the social sciences. If there is an incompatability in notions of reform mechanism between reformers and evaluators, then it should be detected in the advice given by AIR's Technical Review Panel. For that reason the meeting of the panel—as it reacted to a draft section of the *Final Report*—is seen to be crucial and is reported on the following pages (in what one manuscript reviewer called "interminable detail").

The ERS Technical Panel met 9 October 1980 at the Sheraton Hotel in Chicago.[21] Members Robert Perloff, Ward Edwards, Malcolm Klein, Timothy Brock, Lee Sechrest, Edys Quellmalz, and William Cooley joined Charles Murray, Norman Gold, and observers Ernest House and Deborah Trumbull of CIRCE. Tape recordings transcribed ran over 136 pages. Edited excerpts below first include statements on the role of the panel.

---

20. Panel Chairman Perloff called a fifth and final meeting at UCLA (after the final report by AIR was completed) for discussions prior to submitting the ERS report to NIE.

21. During the summer prior to this meeting, to reduce the conflict of interest, I resigned from the Technical Review Panel. I persuaded Chairman Robert Perloff to invite my CIRCE colleagues Ernest House and Deborah Trumbull to attend the Sheraton meeting. They observed and recorded these proceedings.

Brock: The general intent of the Technical Review Panel is to insure objective, critical, scholarly evaluation of AIR's evaluation attempt. ERS would like to establish its credentials for this kind of work for the long-term future. We'd like to be the recipients of additional contracts. We'd like to view ERS as the leading repository of talent and ideas in the evaluation area. So ERS has a stake in doing a very competent job in this particular situation.

Perloff: Our role, I believe, is twofold. One, to provide some kind of expertise, to provide advice which AIR could take as it wishes. Two, to see how this kind of aid, in a dispassionate, objective way, could be used for other large scale evaluation enterprises. By maintaining our integrity, serving as scholars, and giving the best advice we can, we hope that this will be listened to and valued beyond the Cities-in-Schools program.

* * *

Perloff: To an extent we share Charles' frustrations with the program. We also support and endorse the evaluation itself. For CIS and the public, what he did was appropriate. This burden is being shared by us, and therefore Charlie can be less disinclined to be explicit about the results. I think we have the responsibility to get the truth out, while giving encouragement and support.

Sechrest: My conception of the role of ERS is as a quality assurance mechanism which has been previously lacking in program evaluations—in contrast to the way that it exists in "normal science." Careful laboratory studies, peer review of journal articles, and editorial review are examples of quality control mechanisms which are lacking in program evaluations. The enormous consequences (in terms of the amount of money the evaluation is costing and the amount of money the program is costing) demands some form of quality assurance mechanism.

Someone once said that once you've opened a can of worms, the only way to contain it is with a bigger can. And we are the bigger can.

Prior to the meeting Charles Murray had distributed 24 pages entitled "Issues for the CIS Technical Review Panel." Much of this statement appeared later in the *Final Report*. The agenda emphasized three items: assessing the CIS process; assessing the impact of CIS on the students; and institutionalization and replication issues.

According to the agenda announcement, "AIR will present issues and data, while the Panel will be invited to react." This part of the meeting began with a review of the history of Cities-in-Schools by Charles Murray. The response included the following:

Klein: During our first meeting in Indianapolis, we talked about getting data from caseworkers or teachers to learn their response to the *special nature* of the CIS program.

Brock: Are you implying there may have been an "esprit de corps" among the program people?

Klein: There certainly was. You walked through Tech High School and you felt it. In fact when I started to walk out of a classroom, I remember being pigeon-holed by a couple of teachers who were not about to let us walk out of that classroom until they had gotten to us with their view of how important it was and we damn well better understand it. Did you get any of that in the survey data, or did you try for it?

Murray: No. . . and the real question is, can you find that kind of folk in large enough numbers in the program?

* * *

Cooley: I would encourage Charlie to try to figure out what in this set of data is going to suggest some effective things that can be done with these kinds of kids. There are a lot of important things that have been going on that are likely to shed light on the need for inter-agency collaboration, ways in which agencies can increase the likelihood of collaboration, and what caseworkers do that is effective. Every school district has caseworkers, counselors, whatever, and they're all trying to work with this same gang. What worked? Keep that in focus, and forget about trying to "evaluate" CIS—because I think that's a meaningless activity.

Klein: Let me respond, just briefly; social integration of services with the school, the "family" concept, "personalism"—a little collection of ideas that represents a package. That's what they started out with and they have a right to know if it's realistic.

Perloff: We're saying you should do both.

Brock: Can Charlie Murray be called upon to do further analyses about which there is no consensus on this panel?

Perloff: We're an advisory group.

Murray: Well, I'm pretty independent. (Advisory Panel laughter) I'm supposed to have a draft in by November and the final by December and the money's running out. So to some extent I'm looking for guidance. In some cases I'm looking to the panel to say, "It's going to be legitimate if you don't do such and such." I'm looking for excuses not to do certain things, because more could be made of the data, I'm afraid, than I have time to do. So there is a question of priorities.

Voice: (Chuckling) You're going to hang on your own!

Edwards: The message is that in any of these analyses you should not lose sight of the intellectual structure that lies at the core of the CIS idea. Every piece of data that you can look at should be looked at.

* * *

Murray: Let us just assume for a moment that 50 kids were found to show improvement in reading and attendance and that they had a closer relationship than most kids with their caseworkers. How would you decide these better grades and more willingness to participate in school were a function of CIS?

Panel Member: They say to get your data analysis in order is in fact to invent a set of kids for whom you have some invented data and run it through a process. This would lay out a kind of practicum. . . .

Murray: Why do I have to invent them instead of finding them?

Panel Member: If you can find them, great. I'm just saying if you can't.

Murray: I think we'll find them.

\* \* \*

Murray: Suppose we write this up more or less in the terms we used in earlier reports, saying that a program like this really seems justified only for kids who have significant problems, problems that require fairly concrete solutions. Are you folks comfortable with that—given the kinds of data we have?

Perloff: Well, you said earlier it can't be school problems alone.

Murray: Yes, there has to be something beside—either behavioral problems or severe problems in the home that cause reverberations in school.

Panel Member: Do you mean to say that if you do have such students, then, yes, CIS is the right way to go at it? I feel uncomfortable with that.

\* \* \*

Murray: What is the appropriate stance for the report to take regarding the educational outcomes?

Quellmalz: Well, with the test data you have I'm not sure you could tell.

Sechrest: Grades?

Quellmalz: When was the last time you heard that grades were sensitive to much of anything either?

Klein: Well, you've got significant advances in reading scores. The trouble is these are the easiest things to show advances on. I could do it in one half-hour with one of these kids. But you do have the "absentee stuff" which is better.

Quellmalz: You also have the self-report stuff, the kids say, "I think I'm doing better than I was before."

Murray: We also have comparisons where we asked them how they did last year, and which courses they had trouble in. There are radical reductions in certain kinds of problems in courses. That's not matched by grades. It's very soft.

Quellmalz: Was there no attempt to get data that said, "In what ways are you doing things better. On *what* things?" You know if they are better, "How? Why?" Competencies could have been operationalized and measured.

Murray: We could have done a better job in getting indicators of that. We don't have the types of indicators we should have.

Quellmalz: You have nothing to suggest that perhaps there could have been additional benefits? Because they lack sensitivity, the norm-referenced tests wouldn't necessarily pick them up.

Murray: I think the sense of the qualitative is there. I put it in the report.
But when *they* said they were having less difficulty, it meant the difference between being completely baffled and being not *completely* baffled. That the classroom situation was no longer an absolutely negative
experience, frightening and frustrating. They felt like participants in
the class. They had a sense that they were not always being made a fool
of in class.

Edwards: The obvious implication of that, if you take it seriously, is really
outside the scope of the CIS evaluation. But very relevant. Namely,
we're teaching the wrong things to the wrong people.

Murray: The school itself is?

Edwards: Yes, I heard that coming through in various places. Okay, so you
weren't hired to say that, but nevertheless it seems very clear.

\*\*\*

Panel Member: Why are these ideas so difficult to disseminate? How is it
that CIS starts anew and does all of the wrong things all over again? Is
there anyone around there to tell them?

\*\*\*

Panel Member: We can come up with 80 interesting questions, or 8000, that
this study could pursue. You've got to find out who your primary audience is and revisit them. Talk with them, really understand what their
questions are—and then answer them well. Two or three questions . . .
I would like to see us identify maybe twelve big questions, then work
with the agencies' primary target audiences to figure out how these
questions might be refined.

\*\*\*

Panel Member: Why is there such a big difference between the earlier reports on process, which are generally positive, and the later reports on
impact which are negative? The style, affect and tone are very different
in early and later reports.

So here at the close of the study some Technical Review Panelists, especially some new members emphasizing student competencies and causes of outcomes, were telling Murray his data base
was deficient, his choice of variables had been too crude, and even
perhaps that he designed the study poorly. One might infer from the
give and take of this meeting that perhaps he had mismanaged the
job. They apparently were not troubled by the likely possibility that
the job they collectively wanted was not doable.

The panel went into executive session, excluding Murray and
Gold, but not the observers. It was not taped, but the observers made
these notes.

Panel Member: Where is the cause and effect in the analysis? I cannot see the connection between what happened in the program and what the results are.

Panel Member: The standards of the evaluation community certainly are not satisfied by the kinds of analyses done in this evaluation. It is a very unsophisticated study.

Panel Member: The problem is data availability. And earlier on, the evaluators bought the rhetoric of the program people. Now the evaluators are not buying that rhetoric any more, probably as a result of looking at the program.

Panel Member: I think we should submit a list of analyses to be done by the evaluators.

Panel Member: I don't think all those analyses can be done in the remaining time. The data should be in the public domain, with certain proprietary rights exercised by Murray and AIR.

Panel Member: Murray seems exhausted with the project, not wanting to do much else with it. Is there agreement on which analyses should be done. The evaluation faces a problem of integrity.

Other panel members, quiet before, then disagreed. They contended that there were reasons for more faith in AIR's conclusions than in most other studies of this type, that in fact there were important insights to be gained from the evaluation study as it presently stood.

### The Stakeholder Effort

Charles Murray had asked his Technical Review Panel about how to deal with stakeholders, particularly when it became apparent that the demonstration of CIS ideas in these three cities was all too slowly being set up. He increasingly looked to stakeholders to preserve the original intent of the federal experiment. His efforts were portrayed in his "historical summary" (made especially for new panelists) at the Chicago meeting (1980).

Norman Gold set out to make both this evaluation and the PUSH/Excel evaluation "models" of the stakeholder concept. We fell far short of that. We started out defining three different groups of stakeholders. One, the program staff people. Second, the clients of the program, the parents and students themselves. Third, the decision-makers, the people with the money, the people who would decide whether the program would be institutionalized. We further divided the third group into local and national stakeholders. We had one meeting with the national group in the Roosevelt Room at the White House. It was very nice and prestigious—and they were never heard of again. They were just at the meeting because they had been ordered to be there by their cabinet secretaries.

In Atlanta, New York City and Indianapolis we had separate local stakeholder meetings. A lot of very interesting things happened. On the issue of "What constitutes success for you?" we got almost no good ideas. (The review panel suggested we didn't ask the right question—in the right way.) Another element of reactions we got was "Listen, you folks are being paid lots of money to do this and you're supposed to be experts on what constitutes success," and I said to myself, "That's right." (Laughter from those at the meeting). I think if I were in their position and somebody asked me that question I'd say, "No, that's *your* job."

Murray had found the program slow in getting started and shifted his early attention to local CIS program stakeholders. Murray told the panel:

(In the end) the program people were the only *real* stakeholders. We spent a lot of time with them. They would call you and say, "What do you know about this and that and the other thing?" And, "This is what we're doing about that." It was highly interactive. They paid a lot of attention and made changes in the program because of the evaluation. Now, from my perspective, the changes they made in the program were not entirely bright new ideas about what they ought to do. Some came as a result of us saying "Here's what you said you wanted to do. If you still want to do it, we might point out how you are doing it, and suggest a direction move." We did not try to set up a new ideology.

Throughout the three-year study panel members had continued to wonder about stakeholders. The following exchange occurred at the same Chicago meeting (1980) as discussants tried to envision an ideal situation:

Edwards: As stakeholders, how would they work? What would they do? Would they be reading evaluation reports and lobbying?
Gold: No, they'd be talking about the various aspects of the program, deciding which parts they believe in and how relevant or important the program is—and whether anything got left out.
Murray: With Excel, we went knocking on doors. We found the vast majority of parents have very, very, very low interests. It's absurd! The good reaction is that they express a sort of general interest in seeing their kids do well in school. That's the upper half of the reaction. The others felt absolutely powerless to do anything.
Gold: With their unfamiliarity in talking about these issues, it's very frustrating to work with them.
Murray: The school people said, "You want to know what happened the last time we asked the parents to come in? We sat there all night with our tea and donuts—alone. If you want parents then you're going to have to go out and lasso them."
Gold: But the school people did go out and bring the parents in.
Murray: Yes, but what you got was the subset of parents who were fans. We

said to them, "We're from *Washington* and we're *evaluators*. We're going to listen to what you have to tell us about this program." It was a cosmetic attempt at consulting the parents. I think what we were trying to do was to develop "stakeholders" for the evaluation. It's the same thing Jesse Jackson's trying to do in the South. He is trying to get parents to care and to make demands on the school. Jesse Jackson's a lot better at it than we are.

Let's face it, to interview parents in these situations, you have to get highly skilled interviewers who are willing to sit there for three or four hours for maybe two or three minutes of information.

Quellmalz: Do you think the appropriate set of stakeholders would be parents of kids who are being served? What about parents who say, "Hey, why isn't my kid getting this special program?"

Panel Member: How about the parent who says, "This is really terrific. My kid has a better classroom environment because all those other kids (the CIS kids) aren't disrupting the classroom. They're not pushing around so much and beating up my kid."

Quellmalz: You know you have a very wide population of parents who are *not* being served.

Murray: Yes, but now you're getting away from the evaluation.

Perloff: We shouldn't assume the intrinsic validity of the stakeholder process. It's not necessarily a viable concept. It's something that turns Norm on, and NIE. We get people who offer their point of view, their own self interest—and they have the greatest weight.

Murray: The stakeholder idea is very costly both in terms of the time and money you spend on it.

Perloff: There is one other accessible group of stakeholders that you might want to talk to—the teachers.

Murray: Ah, good point. I wish we had treated the teachers as stakeholders. We did include members of the hierarchy of the school district, but not the teachers.

Quellmalz: What about other social service workers who would say, "Gosh, if this program really takes off and I don't look out, I'm going to outstation myself in Siberia," or "This deal is something that's really interesting and will help me be more effective." What about them?

Murray: The data collection on parents and social service workers as stakeholders becomes very thin. We did talk to caseworkers, particularly those who had prior experience in social service agencies to compare the different ways of working and the environments they worked in. We gave them a chance to talk about that, we solicited their views. We did not ask them how we should conduct the evaluation as we did with the stakeholders. We did go out and interview parents about the things in the program they liked or disliked.

There are a lot of different things that people are trying to accomplish through the stakeholder process. Different people make decisions about money and so forth but the most potentially productive use of [the stakeholder approach occurs] by going to the policy-makers.

Gold: We determined the clients a long time ago and we haven't changed. They are people who have a stake in the outcome of this evaluation both at the local and federal levels. There is no priority for the federal level. At the federal level we're really trying to gain greater insight into some of the general issues in education. These issues are of wide-spread interest. But also there are people in these communities who have to make decisions about continuing these programs. This evaluation offered a most disciplined and systematic look at it. We have to remember that Charlie deals not only with the people in this room, but with, for example, the administrators of the Indianapolis Public Schools.

William Cooley continued to seek clarification of the distinction between client and stakeholder.

Cooley: Would you identify them (stakeholders) as the prime clients?
Gold: As an important group. I think the agency people . . . local social ser-
    vices people . . .
Cooley: So, program people, school people . . .
Gold: All these people have been defined as stakeholders. . . .
Cooley: But that's all over the place!

Observer Ernest House had been paying particular attention at these meetings to how the stakeholder concept was treated. He commented:

Murray tended to downplay the stakeholder idea, or else to portray it as somewhat of a failure. Generally I think there is a negative view on behalf of the committee (panel) as a whole. I think Murray himself is not sold on the idea.
    What Murray sees as a true stakeholder group would be something like the PTA. Such doesn't apparently exist in these schools. The way in which AIR tried to engage parents was alien to them.

Once again it is important to note that the panel did not speak in a single voice. Yet there was a consistency to the implication that Murray should provide a record showing what program components contribute to which student gains. As is true of most specialists in program evaluation, these social scientists were "instrumentalists." They were trying to discover the mechanisms and maneuvers to make reform effective. They were interested in stakeholders to understand the limits to which a general CIS program might be considered workable, to know *their* criteria too. There was conflict between the desire for parsimony and the need to acknowledge the heterogeneity of interests and standards. Panelists wanted to know everything (look at all data) but to stick with a few questions done well (for the primary audience) in order to preserve the integrity of the study.

There was little sympathy for Cities-in-Schools, little acknowledgment of its "impossible dream," little empathy for the cities that share these burdens and have so few zealous reformers. That, of course, was not the panelists' assignment.

## The *Final Report*

Draft sections of the *Final Report* were circulated to various stakeholders from September 1980 (the last month of the evaluation three-years) until February 1981. Cities-in-Schools program people were upset with its faint praise. Technical Review Panelists thought it understated the program's failures. The Indianapolis public schools people considered the study an unacceptable departure from traditional statistical study. Though mindful of shortcomings, Norman Gold praised the report. The Reagan administration showed no interest in it.

The report indeed was negotiated. Corrections were made. Room was provided in the appendix for program-staff rebuttal. Objections of several groups were carefully heard and considered in redrafting. In May 1981 about 300 copies of the *Final Report* were distributed to a mailing list of persons who had shown interest during those three years and nine months.

Almost everyone felt disappointment about the evaluation work. Charles Murray was disappointed in the quantity and quality of data at hand and the intransigence of the obstacles to data gathering. Gold was disappointed that almost no one appreciated how well the evaluators had followed the ups and downs of the program, attentive to the disparate needs of stakeholders. Malcolm Klein was disappointed (but mostly with the program), feeling that the idea of "school-based integration of services delivery to reduce juvenile disaffection" had not really been tried. William Milliken felt that the study somehow had "asked" the wrong questions. Superintendent Kalp did not get the third-year impact data he had been promised.

Yet the *Final Report* had much to commend it. First, it presented a most pertinent conclusion about which no one seriously disagreed: that the program generally did not have the intended impact, or even an easily apparent impact, on youth. It presented a detailed statement of program intent. It told briefly of varieties of implementation that occurred at different sites and under different circumstances. It presented information on a few cases (students) considered most successfully served by the program. It examined the obstacles to successful implementation and considered the costs involved. It recommended reconceptualization and reform of government aid if such a youth program is to be effective. It was presented coherently, free of jargon, and with sensitivity to the interests of different stakeholder groups. As a report it was a good report, as were the three reports that preceded it. The arguments against it were with what it did not say and with what apparently the evaluators had not found, more than with what they *had* found.

### The *Final Report* Preparation Process

During stakeholder review of Report 3, the *Impact Report* (on program impact during the first two years), Murray had promised that third-year data would resolve a number of objections. But as indicated on previous pages, the quantitative data originally planned were not delivered in adequate quantity by school district subcontractors. Those test data and attendance records received did not indicate substantial program accomplishment. A subsequent effort to find a cadre of youth clearly rescued by Cities-in-Schools came to naught. Murray found the preparation of the *Final Report* a distressing task.

In October he circulated a rough draft to the Technical Review Panel. The panel was scheduled to meet at the Playboy Club at Lake Geneva, Wisconsin, shortly before election day, but in a show of political sense the meeting was rescheduled at a more staid location, the Sheraton Hotel in Chicago. Commentary from that meeting was presented earlier in this chapter. Panelists urged Murray to indicate forthrightly CIS's failure to create an integrated services system. Also, they said it was important to reiterate that evaluation studies could not be conducted in programs which so consistently resisted regularity, uniformity, and operationalization of impact.

Murray had circulated the draft also to CIS national staff members. They objected strongly to many statements. Joyce McWilliams, CIS evaluation specialist, compiled a list of objections. Burton Chamberlain, Elizabeth Baltz, and McWilliams met at NIE with Murray, Gold, and Kathlyn Moses in March 1981 to iron out misunderstandings. Later, after considering Murray's revisions, McWilliams prepared a rebuttal which AIR included as Appendix A to its *Final Report.* (Still later, McWilliams developed a "Survival Kit" for staff guidance on how to deal with the *Final Report.*)

With pressure from one side to be less severe and from the other to be less sympathetic, the final draft of the AIR report remained almost identical in tone to the original draft. Some parts were amplified; a few words were deleted. The final chapter was rewritten. Now a major share of the blame for ineffective programming was placed on the exigencies of government funding.

One of the most relenting of Murray's changes was removal of the following from the first draft:

*The expectations for using members of the existing social service staffs were not met in any of the three sites.* The figures reveal that only a handful of CIS staff (most in New York, fewest in Indianapolis) were seconded from the regular staffs of existing agencies. (P. 40, first draft.)

and replacing it with the following in the final draft:

*The program did make substantial progress in enlisting the participation of social services agencies.* As shown in Table 3.2 and 3.3, Atlanta and New York were especially successful in obtaining outstationed staff. The large majority of these positions were accompanied by some sort of financial subsidy for the agency.

Not surprisingly, the agency officials who were interviewed consistently reported that their budgets were tightly constrained, and that they could not afford to outstation staff to CIS if the subsidy ended. (P. 48)

Both italicized statements are technically correct and are substantially supported by AIR observations. But this particular substitution lessened the negative side of the report. Had the original version been retained and data presented to support it, the report would have been potentially of greater value to future efforts to integrate social services.

The CIS National Board's strongest objection was to references to the Carters. One member suggested that such political matters were improper topics for evaluators. Murray argued tenaciously that the program could not be understood outside its context. He said CIS evaluators had a professional responsibility to indicate, with propriety, the considerable involvement of the presidential family. He did modify some Carter references, one, for example, from the following sentence: "We may describe the CIS that attracted a short flurry of national publicity, involving a President's special interest in his wife's favored program and (brief) employment for one of the President's sons" (p. 2, *Final Report* Foreword, first draft).

When amended the sentence read: "We may describe the CIS that attracted a short flurry of national publicity because of President and Mrs. Carter's support" (p. 3, *Final Report*).

At the annual meeting of the Evaluation Research Society in October, Murray presented a paper on Cities-in-Schools evaluation but did not indicate what he was writing in the *Final Report*. Partly because the *Impact Reports* had been circulated so recently, and because the Technical Review Panel and CIS people had seen further drafts, audience members expected the report neither would endorse nor condemn CIS. Norman Gold reinforced that view during presentation of his paper, "The Stakeholder Process in Educational Program Evaluation," when he said: "In the CIS evaluation the final report addressing program validation was typically inconclusive. The evaluation, however, has already contributed significantly throughout the previous three years of its life" (16th unnumbered manuscript page, 1981).

Hearing (during the week of that meeting) of the AIR findings, a crestfallen William Milliken wondered again if the right questions had been asked. "Science leaves so much out," he said. Murray remained satisfied that the worthwhile questions had been asked.

Three weeks later the elections were over. Ronald Reagan had won. The Carters would soon leave the White House. A few days later (November 19) Murray presented his findings to Atlanta stakeholders and staff. The meeting was held at the Central Presbyterian Church across the street from the State Capitol. About 15 people attended. The majority were associated with the program or the evaluation. Social amenities were exchanged, but it was not a circle of happy faces around the several tables.

Murray presented his ideas, impressively reasoned and neatly formatted. Copies of his statement on "Atlanta effects only" were distributed. It indicated that services delivery was generally favorable but that "we were unable to detect the effects of the CIS program on its students" (p. 3). Murray orally voiced conclusions on how Cities-in-Schools had not had a chance to succeed—given its uncertain funding, substitution of CETA workers for the expected agency secondments, and different requirements under many different funding arrangements. He addressed at length the reasons the program did not succeed, considering it apparent that it had not succeeded. The discussion included this exchange:

Unidentified: Chuck, you examined the different goals we have and the activities to achieve these objectives?

Murray: Yes.

Unidentified: Did the program conduct these activities?

Murray: The program looked pretty good with regard to carrying out the activities it said it would. In some Atlanta sites the reading curriculum was not as strong as it should have been. The orientation class was not as strong as it was at some other places. By and large I think the program has done quite well.

Unidentified: Has there been any success with the original concept of 10 students to one teacher or professional? Can you rearrange the assignments of professionals to deal at a more concentrated level with the students?

Murray: Atlanta got a start with that. At Smith there was a sworn police officer—two at one point. And a staff member from the Department of Children and Family Services. So the answer to your question is, "No, it has not been fully implemented." Whole staffs of agencies are not being sent out, decentralized. But when you have these kinds of people in the schools, it has worked out the way Bill Milliken said it would. They have proved to be time-savers and waste-cutters. They get things done. So that has worked.

Murray answered many questions about "outstationing" personnel. He repeated indication of things that had gone well. But he emphasized overall that these arrangements had not resulted in *measurable improvement* in the behavior of the youth.

David Lewis, city director for CIS in Atlanta, challenged Murray on the evidence of failure at Smith High School and noted that Project Director Jimmy Hardy had identified numerous youngsters who greatly benefited. Murray carefully detailed the AIR search through files for evidence to support the claims, concluding that they could not be sustained in even a majority of "most favorable" cases. Angry, Lewis asked if Murray would have reported it the same had the Democrats won. Murray replied that the findings had been prepared well before the election and that he was deeply offended by the insinuation.

The meeting was as much a confrontation as it was a presentation of information to satisfy user needs. Some of the evaluator's findings were debatable and program people debated him. (In Indianapolis it had been the district staff which debated him.) Here only a few non-CIS stakeholders spoke up. Henry Zimmer, head of planning of the United Way, asked for clarification of a few points and expressed need for more information. Murray indicated that more could be available in the full report in a couple of months.

By March 1981 Murray had made the round of stakeholders and had the CIS rebuttal in hand, along with reactions from several members of the Technical Review Panel and from AIR colleague Robert Krug. Krug's memo said that some of the conclusions drawn (e.g., better trained caseworkers were needed, the curricular offerings were poorly coordinated) were not adequately supported by data presented. He closed with this admonition:

Some of the things you said in your paper to the Technical Review Panel seem very true. You liked the people and you wanted the CIS to work. I truly believe that you have leaned over backward farther than you should. In wanting to save the baby, you were unwilling to throw out the bathwater and I believe it should be thrown. By all means, emphasize the positive. But divorce these positive elements from the excess baggage with which CIS, the program, burdened them. At least consider it. (P. 4, 2 February 1981.)

Murray rewrote the conclusions chapter, increasing emphasis on the debilitating nature of the funding, de-emphasizing assessment of program components and such key internal issues as "Should CIS continue to pursue a separate educational component, or leave education to the school?" Murray wanted to address the process concerns of stakeholders more directly, but data gathering had not been successful enough to permit it.

The *Final Report* was published in May 1981. About 300 copies were circulated by Norman Gold to a mailing list of people who had participated or had shown interest in the evaluation work. A few months later the supply was exhausted and copies were available neither from AIR nor NIE.[22] Even with NIE taking massive budget cuts, an effort was started to review the evaluation methodology, but no funds were available for further dissemination of the report.

The Findings

Considerable wisdom was embodied in the *Final Report* by drawing attention to the numerous perspectives people had on Cities-in-Schools, not only on how well it worked but even on what it was.

---

22. The *Final Report* can be purchased from the ERIC Document Reproduction Service, P.O. Box 190, Arlington, Va. 22210 (ED 210 360: 214 pages, paper copy $15.20, microfiche $.91, at the time this is being written). It also exists in numerous depositories.

Charles Murray recognized that a somewhat different, yet accurate, final report could have been written from any of several perspectives. He noted the choices, in terms of stakeholders:

We may describe the CIS that the supporters of CIS see: a small group of dedicated street workers with one of the few original approaches available.

We may describe the CIS that attracted a short flurry of national publicity because of President and Mrs. Carter's support.

We may describe the CIS of the social worker and youth counselor, who point to the intrinsic value of the services that CIS provides.

We may describe the CIS that was portrayed by officials of the existing social service and school systems, of amateurs who are long on rhetoric and short on performance.

We may describe the CIS that the CIS staff sees: an underfunded, hand-to-mouth effort that is trying to tackle some of the most intractable of our urban problems while fighting off bureaucratic interference and rivalries.

Each of these versions can be sustained by the facts. CIS did some things very well and some things very badly. Depending on how one values the different things, CIS can be seen as an extravagance or a necessity (p. 3).

Murray chose to present three approaches: a contextual evaluation (Chapter Two), a traditional program evaluation (Chapter Three), and a diagnostic section indicating "what has been learned" (Chapter Four). The final chapter was devoted to conclusions and began as shown in Figure 8.

Murray's basic conclusion was that the program was not cost-effective. He based that conclusion not so much on a comparison with other delivery systems or on an analysis of costs but on the fact that good effects had generally not been demonstrated for the portion of the millions spent that could be considered ordinary operating cost.

Notwithstanding the contrary views of people affiliated with the program, CIS evaluation data gatherers, analysts, and others confirmed this impression: good effects were not visible. The program people protested: their experience told them of continuous and substantial benefit to the youngsters. But they did not have "data" to back it up.

A reader of the *Final Report* was not encouraged there to think that a pro-CIS case still might be made in spite of the findings. No attention was given the possibility. A key sentence in the middle of page 111 (see Figure 8) said: "The best that can be argued from the

# Chapter V.

## Conclusions

The final step in any evaluation is to try to synthesize the evidence that was assembled, to make one or more summative statements about the program's value. In the case of CIS, this can be done at several levels. If the summative question is the simplest one,

> "Is the program as it exists a good invest-
> ment of public funds?"

the answer from the three sites that we examined is "no." In one year, in one site (Indianapolis in 1978-79), the program could point to evidence of a pattern of positive results. Elsewhere, and in other years, the program did not demonstrably affect the behavior of large numbers of its participants. The best that can be argued from the record is that perhaps things would have been even worse without CIS. Lacking adequate comparison groups, that possibility remains open. The data that bear on the issue cast doubt on that proposition.

At the next level, the question becomes,

> "Can the factors that limited the program's
> effectiveness be corrected?"

Three types of impediments limited CIS's results: The way the program was funded and structured by its sponsors, the way the program was run by its administrators, and the responses of local agencies and school systems.

Of these three, the dominant factor was the funding arrangements. Even if the other problems had not existed, the program's ability to implement the planned CIS would have been crippled. The most important impediments were:

111

Figure 8. Conclusions, AIR *Final Report.*

Source: *The National Evaluation of the Cities-in-Schools Program. Report No. 4: Final Report* (1981), p. 111.

record is that perhaps things would have been even worse without CIS." That is not quite true. Looking at the record accumulated by AIR, one could more generously say, "It can be argued from the record that the extended interactions between caseworkers and youth will pay off in ways not indicated in this record." The record was not definitive. Indeed, it was poor. It was poor partly because of low-quality data gathering and partly because such gains as there were in attendance, achievement, and lawfulness appeared neither substantial nor enduring. Whatever the *actual* accomplishment of Cities-in-Schools, it remained poorly known.[23] What is known is that it fell greatly below promises and expectations. Murray's conclusion as to cost-effectiveness—based on pre-specified and at-the-time agreed-upon criteria—was surely correct.

Gathered from pages across his Chapter Three, the accomplishments of CIS can be seen centered on assertions regarding programmatic processes, impact on youth, and ability to remain within existing costs for services delivery.[24] As to the "provision of a superior structure and process for integrated service delivery to disadvantaged youngsters," the *Report* presented these conclusions:

CIS did deal for the most part with students having serious, probably multiple problems (p. 43).

Expectations for the training and expertise of caseworkers were not met in any of the three sites (p. 47).

The program did make substantial progress in enlisting the participation of social service agencies (p. 48).

Caseworkers developed close personal relationships, usually at the school setting and regarding school topics, with some of the CIS students needing it, but clearly not all (p. 48).

Expectations to monitor schoolwork and follow-up absences were met. Efforts to provide remedial help varied from intensive to fragmentary (p. 55).

Caseworkers provided a good range of enrichment activities but student participation fell off during the third year of observation (p. 57).

---

23. I wrote in the margin of my interview notes: "Sometimes one waits up until a daughter comes home. But sometimes one goes looking for her. Charlie was watching to see if the program had made it home."

24. Murray originally expected to include here a fourth assertion regarding feasibility of the CIS model for dissemination to other cities, but chose to subsume that under concerns about federal support, the central idea of the final chapter.

CIS caseworkers seldom reported orchestration of service delivery to meet family-specific needs (p. 62).

The program staff disagreed vigorously only with the last conclusion (see rebuttal, *Final Report*, Appendix A). The issue of staff competence had been compromised when CIS decided to accept large numbers of CETA workers as caseworkers. CIS apparently had no grand plan for identifying service agencies which should have been integrated, but AIR gave little attention to identifying agencies that should have been integrated but were not.

The evaluators also chose not to evaluate CIS emphasis on academic tasks as the basis for caseworker-student interaction, nor to question omission of vocational training. The list of assertions above followed the conceptual organization set by CIS. The evaluators had more issues to raise than the CIS people were interested in having raised. Given the considerable organizational difficulties within and across projects, the AIR evaluators restricted themselves to a number of topics they more or less unobtrusively could ask questions about. A more elaborate list of process issues could have been investigated.

Having made few independent observations, the evaluators were dependent on CIS caseworkers' records for "data on services delivered." As a group these people had been found inadequately trained in teaching, counseling, and personal problem solving. They were no better at record keeping. Burton Chamberlain and other CIS leaders claimed (see Chamberlain quotation next chapter) that staff members were reluctant to cooperate with the evaluators, possibly to the extent that they even "boycotted" some of the evaluation work.[25] For assessing *services delivered*[26] the dependence of AIR on CIS logs is indicated in the *Final Report*: ". . . AIR's numbers were

---

25. Noncooperation might be expected to grow into self-enhancing falsification of the accounting system. But no instance of falsification was reported by the evaluators, and only one witness interviewed for this meta-evaluation study reported falsification. Of course interviewees often offered anecdotes which favored their advocacy or opposition to the program.

26. To some people "services delivered" translates into "information provided." Murray rejected a stereotypic view that poor people needed information about the welfare services available: "The popular image of needs out there is not quite right. In fact, most folks do know about Medicaid. They know about welfare payments. In fact, they are quite sophisticated about the welfare system. Many times you have caseworkers who say they

obtained throughout an extremely detailed examination of the files. Instructions were explicit that every possible instance be noted. The data collectors independently reviewed identical files on a spot-check basis. Two data collectors always worked together, so that marginal items could be discussed" (p. 86).

The evaluators had respectable criteria for rejecting many of the retrospective CIS claims that the logs showed much more service than AIR acknowledged. But AIR had no quality-control information to dismiss possible underreporting of assistance to youth. These potential data almost surely would not have changed the AIR findings of "little accomplishment," but they might have supported a different argument of what urban social services should accomplish.

As to *costs*, Murray claimed that much of the cost of Cities-in-Schools here—because it was an innovative effort operating under deadlines, because it was under scrutiny, because money was there to be spent—should not be considered part of the ordinary operating expense of a Cities-in-Schools operation. He provided bases for a potential user to estimate what the local costs might be, noting that these costs would vary with certain important options, such as whether or not the "outstationed" agency personnel were people of long experience or recently employed. For one set of contingencies Murray estimated the cost per student per year to be just over $2,000. IIe devoted little attention to analyzing the actual costs of CIS in Atlanta, New York, and Indianapolis, not only because he saw them as of little general knowledge value but also because they were very difficult to obtain and of questionable accuracy.[27]

The AIR effort to measure *impact on youth* was greatly hampered by the movement of youngsters in and out of the program and the failure of caseworkers and others to update identification of who came to any event. His base group in the three high schools numbered about 200 students. Each site had about a 30 percent annual attrition from school rosters. Murray was reluctant to do the planned analyses, given such incomplete records of attendance, achieve-

---

identify such and such a need, but the mother has already gone to such and such an office to get it. Only a small number of folks out there have needs that could be matched by existing services they don't already know about" (comment to Technical Review Panel).

27. I never asked Murray why good impact results would be generalizable but good cost figures would not.

ment, and reduction of delinquency. "Cell sizes were too small and comparability across cells was questionable."

Murray stressed the limits of the comparisons he presented but did conclude that "students with attendance problems in the ninth grade behaved [attended school] about the same in the tenth grade whether or not they were in CIS." He went on to say, "The main point does not have to do with attendance but with the magnitude of distortions introduced into all of the impact measures by the large attrition rate . . . . Even ignoring the selection problem, the numbers as they stand are not generally positive. Grades for example did not increase even among those who remained in school; in fact, they declined slightly over the students' first two years in the program. The items covered for 1978–79 in *Report No. 3* (e.g., on values, difficulty in school, focus of control, level of effort) did not reveal improvements among students who remained in the program." He concluded the section on impact with: ". . . the quantitative analysis of impact revealed no consistent pattern of progress in New York and Atlanta for either of the two years 1978–79 and 1979–80. The analysis did show a consistent pattern of positive indicators in Indianapolis for the 1978–79 school year. This pattern was not repeated in 1979–80. The parsimonious explanation is that the 1978–79 program was not repeated in the subsequent year, because of the teachers' strike and understaffing" (pp. 79–81).

Although he had few hard data which would support the continuation of the Cities-in-Schools program, Charles Murray considered his three-year immersion in these urban schools to justify concluding the *Final Report* on this positive note:

Maybe nothing will work by the time that adolescence is reached, and programs will have to focus on the earlier years. But if the choice is to keep trying, then the lesson of the CIS evaluation is not to toss CIS aside and hope for something better. The more reasonable assumption is that "an inner-city school that works will include as part of its resources something very much like CIS, and that the most economical way to reach that goal is to build on the start that CIS has made. (P. 120, *Final Report*.)

### Subsequent Events

After completing the *Final Report*, Charles Murray resigned from the American Institutes for Research. President Schwarz urged him to continue in some capacity, guaranteeing consultation assignments. Murray turned to writing political analysis and fiction. At AIR his next big project was to have been an overview of what has been learned by social scientists about urban support programs. In 1984 he did publish *Losing Ground*, extending his doubts about federal capacity to support social reform (dwelt on in the last chapter of the CIS final report). As reported by the *Wall Street Journal* (Sept. 17, 1985), the book became a frequent citation in political arguments about dismantling federal social programs.

The Cities-in-Schools projects met with various fates. As a result of aggressive promotion by the national board and backing from the mayor's office, activity in New York City was extended to District 12 in the Bronx where 60 city social service staff workers (primarily from the Human Resources Administration) were reassigned to the schools. An additional four were provided by private funding. The projects in Atlanta continued at Smith High School and at all but one of the street academies. A new one was opened in the fall of 1982 with Rich's Department Store as host. The projects in Indianapolis were essentially discontinued, but members of the Policy Group (stakeholders group) there appealed to the new superintendent to reinstate the program. Projects continued in Houston, Oakland, and Washington. New starts were begun in 1982 in Bethlehem, Pennsylvania, and Los Angeles, the latter something of a successor to the PUSH/Excel effort there.

The Technical Review Panel met on one subsequent occasion to consider retrospectively what the panel had contributed to the evaluation work. The National Institute of Education itself was threatened with termination by the Reagan people. It remained, but neither in size nor security. Norman Gold was put into termination status there, but in early 1983 was returned to his position. Kathlyn Moses retired from her position as director of urban initiatives and was not replaced.

The CIS National Office closed in midsummer 1983.

# 4

## Contrasting Views of the Evaluation Study

For this review, the evaluation study is *figure* against a *ground* of complex program activity. For the program people, of course, the evaluation study was part of the diverse and sometimes chaotic background. The reactivity of the evaluation work can better be understood by examining the views of various stakeholders. I personally conducted the interviews. First I will present a selection of statements from CIS people.

### William Milliken and Other CIS People

I talked to William Milliken and others on several occasions to learn how they felt the evaluation study affected CIS. The interviews expanded, revealing how they felt about the program and many contemporary problems.

WILLIAM MILLIKEN: President and co-founder of Cities-in-Schools, Atlanta. Excerpts from an interview, May 1982.

Stake: Bill, have you run into potential funders who said, "No, the evaluation *Final Report* said you aren't good enough to get support?"

Milliken: No. Well, one maybe. We were getting jammed, and I didn't know it. It took me two years to uncover where it was coming from. Anyhow I found the guy who was doing it, a very powerful person. I went in eyeball-to-eyeball and just said, "Hey, look, I just want to know. If we're doing something wrong, just tell me." It ended up just being a personal conflict, out of the past.

But he had really studied the Reports. When I came in he knew that I was going to shoot straight so he was prepared with every quote.

99

I just said, "Hey, I can prove this and this. They're right there. This I don't agree with." And we went through the thing. We ended up getting our first grant from them. That was the only place where anyone used it against us.

Stake: Most of your people say that the evaluation did help you resolve some problems internally. So in that way, there was some value to it. But that the findings were information you already knew. The expected big payoff wasn't there. Do you agree?

Milliken: I would say yes to all of that. It has been more than a little help internally. We got our first unqualified audit. We were able to convince the Board to help us. It got us money for a Resource Center in Washington. The part on structural management, the students, all that stuff, was very helpful.

We've got a system in place now. We aren't getting criticized. That has helped us in fund raising. If somebody wants to give you money and you're unorganized they'll help you to get organized. If you don't then that's the first thing they'll jam you on. If you've got that covered, then they have to deal with program. We had both blanks uncovered. We were just offering an idea at that time. Now we have something we can show people.

If it were strictly an internal evaluation I would throw out two parts of it. I am at a prejudice point—even more than I was before. I don't know how people who haven't been through this [can understand CIS]. I think I could do a better evaluation of a program like this because I've had that out there. I see a cultural problem, a jaundiced way of looking. I think I've had that suspicion all along. I don't know how any human being could do it. I don't know how you evaluate it. Who doesn't come with their own political bias, in the broadest sense? Their own background? If I'm a liberal and I'm evaluating, I'm going to be more biased that way. If I'm coming out of a more conservative experience then I'd be more that way.

Stake: Did you feel that stronger after you read *Time* magazine's piece on Charlie Murray's political views?

Milliken: Yes, I think I did feel stronger about it. That may have been what made the lights go on, but I had said this to him during the process. I guess that's what bothers me about evaluation. I'm almost convinced in any of these education evaluations, it is "an outsider looking in." From my viewpoint the whole scientific method seems screwy. Take out all the variables and look at the whole thing. It's almost as if they say, "You've got to to build a community, but do it piece by piece without looking at the community to see how the various pieces work within it."

Stake: Kathy tells me that you're still running into lots of resentment against evaluators here. So why do you put up with this sort of thing? Is it because your chairman, Howard Samuels, believes in it? I'm wondering whether you feel evaluation work is going to be a wasted expense.

Milliken: The reason I smiled is that the last meeting I had in New York was with Howard. Howard talked of evaluation. He's not talking like you or Charlie would be talking about evaluation. He is looking at it as management. He's looking strictly at that side of the ledger. He is the most humane . . . he cares whether that kid turns around and whether he ever learns anything. Is he hurting anybody or hurting himself? Is he going to end up driving a truck and taking care of his family? I think when Howard reads an evaluation you'll hear him pop off the same philosophical thing. But if we say we're increasing attendance he wants to make sure we're increasing attendance. Are the majority of them going to get marketable skills? He wants to know that. He's looking at it as a line boss. The bottom line is productivity.

Stake: Neil was speaking yesterday about a kid who finally *initiated* communication with a caseworker after a year involvement. It was the first sign of a "turnaround." Well, every kid is going to have his own way. . . .

Milliken: That's right. It's so different with different kids. I had a guy sitting there, just before you came in. He walked through that door . . . once he'd lived across from me. He was a person I was dealing with when I was first here, had a hard time breaking through. He murdered a person and was sent away. I'd go in to visit him. Now he was sitting there today, ready to communicate. How do you evaluate what happened over the past eight years? Because of that turnabout he is working, supporting his family. This guy, you know . . . the walls were so thick!

Stake: When you talked to me during the Evaluation Society meeting in Arlington you were very upset by Murray's findings. You said, "I wonder if they're asking the right questions." When Charlie hears you saying that, he gets exasperated. He says, "But we asked and we asked. We asked what the right questions were. What else should we be looking for? And they either said they didn't know or they mentioned things that we were already looking at."

Milliken: I don't know how to respond to that. If I were in his shoes, and felt that way, I'd be exasperated too.

Milliken did not accept the negative conclusions of Murray's evaluation report. He denied them, wondering aloud how Murray could be expected to understand, "outsider" that he was. The "Truth" had to do with youth who overcome the scars of murder, overcoming social walls "so thick." In closing he expressed empathy for anyone who sees things the researcher's way.

ELIZABETH BALTZ: Once city director of Cities-in-Schools, Indianapolis; later federal coordinator on the CIS national staff officed in Washington. Here we have excerpts from a November 1981 interview. Baltz by then was a graduate student at Columbia University.

Baltz: It is a problem to evaluate any program like this. You don't know what the kids are going to be doing in five years. This program is having more impact than we think. These kids have had problems all through their first eight years of school. They might have some significant gains but it may take four years, not one or two years, for the results to show up. It's a hard thing to measure.

AIR was trying very hard. They did what they could with it, but still it was frustrating. You see a good program, with all these obstacles, being evaluated on these criteria—that we're all agreed on, but . . . I don't know.

There should have been more comparing costs of the program against the costs if these kids were incarcerated. One needs a broader perspective than "This is just a little program and it works or it doesn't work." We're dealing with more than that. One needs the bigger picture and less of the technical . . . a little more about what a good Cities-in-Schools program could mean. It was left: maybe CIS was working and maybe not?

Stake: Betsy, I thought Charlie was surprisingly supportive of the program in the beginning and surprisingly detached in the end; perhaps regretful that he had become so personally attached to the problems of the program, wanting to be the dispassionate scientist at the very end. It occurred to some people that Charlie's disaffection might be related to the results of the national election. More conservative people were now in power.

Baltz: I don't believe that at all. Personally I have great respect for Charlie. I think he's excellent at what he does. Charlie tried very hard to be objective.

JOYCE McWILLIAMS: Director of evaluation, CIS national office, Atlanta. August 1982.

Asked how CIS leaders responded to AIR evaluation reporting, McWilliams said, "At first there would be a flurry of concern. They would go over the words, objecting to some, recommending corrections. No one ignored it; some looked for ways of improving things and others looked for ways of neutralizing its effect." She did not see indications that as a result, the reform effort "quieted."

In correspondence, McWilliams spoke of the good effects AIR had on CIS:

1. CIS National Office became able to legitimatize internal evaluation.
2. Created climate hospitable to development of a national evaluation plan.
3. Assisted development of "Affiliate Agreements" with the CIS cities.

BURTON CHAMBERLAIN: Executive vice-president, Cities-in-Schools, Atlanta. Excerpts from an interview, May 1982.

Chamberlain: You asked me if the AIR report captured the essence of CIS. I would say "Maybe 60%." If I had been in this National CIS office from the beginning, with part of the ownership of the design, with historical participation in it, I think both the application and the implications of the study would have had more meaning.

But the study, as a management tool and as something to look at, as a prism for evaluating the program . . . it still has great value. I look at it as a vehicle that has forced the CIS organization to see evaluation as critical to its survival.

When the City Directors and our national management looked at the evaluation it was an ordeal. Now I think of "the ordeal" in a different perspective. If you superimpose evaluation from outside it is used by the outside to enforce the rules. It can be part of local management-design. I think that's where we're moving, finding how to utilize the organization's strengths. So evaluation is no longer a battle.

Over the two year period suspicion had been building up about Charlie's motivation, about AIR's motivation, about their cultural perspectives. At some point, AIR—whether it was personalized in Charlie, or whether it was just Charlie—was seen as someone other than an ally to the cause, to get black children saved and put back into society. That was not unilateral but it certainly took place in the cities.

Personalities always affect the results of the action. Murray's main link in our organization was Betsy. Betsy was seen as persona non grata [by some people] in this organization. So if Betsy was the one feeding Charlie much of the information it was seen as distorted. If Charlie was listening to Betsy then [the AIR interpretation] wouldn't be favorable; [wouldn't be] what was really going on in our cities. A lot of these things entered into the pot and clouded the perceptions of the City Directors. This puts a value on how important the information is.

Sometimes the City Directors may say to project directors, "I want these data gathered"—but by their body posture and what they're saying outside, it's not putting a priority on it.

Would I say there was a boycott of the evaluation effort? It's a strong word but . . . (long pause) . . . it's close to it. Close to it.

Among these several CIS people the feeling was strong that their views of reality were not presented by the evaluators, and possibly not even seen. The CIS people had their own differences to deal with. In a sense the evaluation gave them a common foe.

DAVID LEWIS: President of Exodus Inc.; member of the board of directors of CIS; city director of Cities-in-Schools, Atlanta. Excerpts from an interview, May 1982.

Lewis: At the outset, the right tools for evaluation were not there. It was probably our fault as much as theirs. We were naive. We felt that here was a group of evaluators coming in to assess what we were doing and from that to develop some kind of tool to decide how effective it was. It was hard in the beginning to do that because the people who were doing the evaluation wanted the people who they were evaluating, the kids and the staff, to talk. Once they got to the point they could talk honestly with a person, that person was gone, and in came another person.

We paid enough for that evaluation to have been given more time than we got, to have gained more insight into what we were doing. If the evaluation had come out negative, well and good. If we weren't doing the thing . . . but at least give us the benefit of the doubt and tell us, "Hey, you're not doing this. Here's what you're doing."

People in evaluation don't have enough time to really look at what's happening with people who are in the most dire need. Two people on a research evaluation team make as much money as ten people who are trying to serve those people, help remotivate those people. I think something is wrong.

Some people became aware of Charlie Murray's evaluation work in Chicago.[1] They said, "In the final analysis, what Charlie Murray had said was that rather than try to help some young people who were probably destined for prison, 'that' might be better for them than trying to help them move back into the mainstream of society." So right away people were a little leery: "What are they going to do with what I'm going to say? What are they going to do with this study? What are they going to do with our kids? Should I actually give them this information. Will it be made public? How much can I trust them?"

I would tell staff people, "Hey, I want you to talk to the evaluators. Just tell how you do things, your counseling methods, your home visits, how you conduct your plans." They say, "Hey, do I have to talk to them? Why the hell should I tell them anything? They just come down to use us for guinea pigs. Why should I?"

The stakeholder approach was good. But if you take the head of a social agency who has to run his or her own social agency every day, there's going to be very little that they can tell you intelligently about any of the workings. All they see is the wash when it comes out of the machine or when it's hung up to dry. They don't know what kind of bleach you used or what you put into the machine.

Some people thought that the evaluation didn't do the program justice. Some who were involved had seen the kids coming through the program. They'd seen the changes in the kids. They said to us, "you're being had."

NEIL SHORTHOUSE: Assistant director of Exodus, Atlanta. Excerpts from an interview, May 1982.

Shorthouse: I just don't believe there wasn't a substantial number of kids on which an impact was made. If Dave Lewis or I wanted to, we could interview every one of those kids over at Academy today, asking, "Tell me

---

1. A reference to the UDIS study mentioned in the Chapter Three section on staffing.

about the program. What do you think about it? Is it doing anything for you?" I would bet anything that 90% of the kids would say: "There's something happening here. I need to be in on it. That's why I'm here. I think I'm making some progress with it."

If everything that Charlie did was accurate (and he did get basically "no results") Jim Hardy would say, "Well, it isn't because we didn't try. Maybe something will happen later, but in that much time we just couldn't pull it off with these kids. They were just in too bad shape when we got them." Smith was well organized. Jimmy was a good manager. He stayed on those people. They knew what they were supposed to do. They did the home visits. They worked their asses off. I don't know the answer, but it was not because it was disorganized. I do believe that disorganization sabotaged agency coordination. I just don't know why he couldn't come up with that data (pause), assuming that the data was as he found it.

I think some things were happening in these kids' lives, altering them, for the better, certainly in the majority of cases. I mean, our kids' grade-levels bottomed out—then the slide stopped. Our kids' grades were going up, slowly. Maybe a grade-level a year in math and reading.

Charlie didn't study the street academies much, mainly because he didn't think the records were sufficient. Our people in the street academies came with a desire to work with kids, to spend time with kids. They weren't paperwork types. But they needed to be. Paperwork is not all bad. But that's why Charlie couldn't do much with the street academies.

WILLIAM SMITH: City director of Cities-in-Schools, Indianapolis. Excerpts from an interview with Robert Stake and Deborah Trumbull, December 1981.

William Smith said that the AIR study indicated a few things not already known, but for the most part it was useful because it did confirm important things they already knew. He said he was disappointed that so little time was spent trying to understand the attitudes of the youngsters and what is happening in their lives. He said he understood the limitations of measurement that AIR faced, but felt the questions asked were too attentive to what the administrators were doing. Smith also stated that the last year of data gathering seemed incomplete. The only data gathering he knew of was done by Charles Murray, Blair Bourque, and Toni Simons: "Toni did most of it, Blair a little, and Charlie went to meetings." He recalled there had been problems with the schools being unwilling to release some of the information, probably because the information was not highly accurate and potentially embarrassing to the schools.

BRUCE SPRAGGINS: Assistant to the city director, Cities-in-Schools, New York City. Excerpts from an interview, July 1981.

Spraggins did not see that the *Final Report* had any major problems. He said that the balance of attention among student impact, teacher issues, and administration problems was suitable. According to Spraggins, the AIR report gave him some information he could use, but not a lot. He said information about the personal help students get on a one-on-one basis was missing.

CAROLYN SMITH: City co-director, South Bronx Project, New York City. Excerpts from an interview, July 1981.

Smith: The Bronx was not really part of the evaluation. Julia Richman High School was used. Julia Richman was separated from the community because of its placement, and this made it very hard for the school to exhibit a dynamic or a heavy interest in Cities-in-Schools. The Bronx had a lot happening because we were in the schools and the community. There was a dedication and ownership—a striving—that went into the Bronx programs, and the atmosphere was conveyed through any staff member we had. We had staff who would get out there and work until 9:00 at night with no money for that time. So the spark, the interest, the activity, the momentum, to my knowledge, that contributed to the growth and dynamics of the program really came out of the Bronx program. I felt that that was left out of the evaluation.

I feel that AIR got really bogged down in the beginning stages with the administrative things, and they never got out of it. I feel that we made a great move and a great change rather suddenly and AIR never really caught up with it. They were really still at the beginning of the program.

I know that Charlie was making trips to New York constantly for a while and then dropped off. I think that Harv Oostdyk and Charlie had some long discussions. I think that a lot of discouragement and disillusionment happened to AIR through Charlie. You see, Charlie would come in and sit down and talk with Harv who would tell him about all the ideas going around in his head. That wasn't really what was going on in the field. I heard quite a lot of things from Charlie Murray about things that were supposed to be happening that were not happening in New York. I think that's a key element to some things over all about AIR's approach to the evaluation. I told Charlie in an open meeting, "A lot of things you're speaking about and complaining about aren't happening in the field." He then said, "Well, Harv says they are." I don't know how you solve this problem.

After the early concentration I saw the AIR focus going on to some internal conflicts between a few of our top people. I saw a lack of consistency in terms of people on site, not really sticking to determining which way to go in evaluating the program itself. I think things were discouraging to AIR. What they thought was going on was not going on in the field. I think there was much more substance in the field than AIR grasped.

KATHLEEN MAXWELL: Evaluation specialist, Exodus, Inc., Atlanta. Excerpts from an interview, May 1982.

Maxwell: The AIR evaluation was too early. We would have been in much better shape if the evaluation had been done today.

AIR changed who was responsible for gathering data in Atlanta. Jane Schubert was great. She was setting it up right. Then she was gone. Saundra Murray was a great person, but quickly got overloaded. One of the local interviewers didn't have rapport and wasn't acceptable. We wanted advance information about what the evaluation people would be doing so that we could get people to cooperate. It did not work to give them general instructions a month in advance. We had to brief them just before the encounter. We needed to sell the idea of the evaluation to our projects and the project people had to sell it to the students. People were defensive.

AIR wanted success to show up in jobs, grades and graduation. That is totally unrealistic. A student fails to do a test because his Dad makes him go pay a bill. You have to be creative in finding success. Many kinds of success are hard to mark on a chart. Removal of hostility, for example.

SARAH DAVIS: an unemployed teacher hired through CETA as a CIS tutor in Indianapolis in 1977–79.

Davis: I went along with the CIS management information system enough to assure myself that I was accountable. Some people took it as a joke. Everyone complained about it.

Stake: We are talking about the record-keeping system installed the second year? It wasn't part of your work the first year, right?

Davis: That's right. It wasn't something you would overlook. There were sheets for achievement, and sheets for social development, and others.

Stake: Didn't you feel that information needed to be recorded?

Davis: Not all of it applied. My youngsters needed help with math. I didn't do much besides tutoring. The sheets may have been appropriate for Tech but they weren't for us.

Stake: So you objected? Why?

Davis: Well, it was burdensome. It did not seem important partly because of the irregularity. Sometimes they had to have them the next day. Sometimes not until the next week. Sometimes a group leader would treat them as important, other times not.

Stake: So sometimes you kept them and sometimes you didn't?

Davis: No, I always kept the parts pertinent to the tutoring. Some of us did, others did not. A lot of them were not professional about anything. They didn't know what it was all about. Some didn't care.

Stake: About the record keeping or about the kids?

Davis: Some didn't care about either one. But the unprofessional ones mostly just did things their own way. And some of it was pretty bad.

Stake: What do you mean?

Davis: Well, they would manipulate kids. They probably didn't hurt anyone. They did cause a division in the staff. Some were pretty racist. I'm sure some weren't aware of what they were doing. Mostly they were not enabling the kids to grow—making the kids more dependent, not less dependent but more dependent on them.

Stake: Wasn't there training for them?

Davis: Very little.

Stake: Did they falsify records?

Davis: Yes, it wasn't uncommon. People cheated.

Stake: Are you sure? Did you see it yourself?

Davis: Yes.

Stake: I heard it said that some of the CETA workers needed the social services more than the kids they were caring for. Is that possible?

Davis: I think it was true.

Stake: Do you think any of them were actually out to sabotage the system?

Davis: Some talked about boycotting it. Don't get me wrong. There were some really good people working in the program. The person I worked for was exceptional. He would say, "I'm doing my job. I do not need to make a home visit that many times a month. They can fire me." Sometimes he did crazy things, but he provided the resources a child needed.

Stake: Was he offended by the evaluation?

Davis: People I was with did not really come in contact with the outside evaluators. Remember, I wasn't at Tech. We quickly got the feeling that only the Tech program was important.

Stake: Did you know Betsy Baltz? She got a lot of credit for getting the management information system going. Was she doing a good job?

Davis: I knew who she was. I didn't think she was very consistent. She didn't seem to have reasons for some of the things she did. I know she was working under pressure. But the biggest pressure seemed to be to get something going that would make Harv look good.

Stake: So people who saw it that way were not highly inclined to make the record system work?

Davis: I had mixed emotions. A lot of people did not understand that they needed to be accountable in some written form. They just saw it as something Tech said we had to do.

Stake: You saw the obligations as coming from Tech?

Davis: Yes.

Stake: What was your main gripe?

Davis: The money maybe. Some of these people were getting a lot of money and I was getting almost nothing. I was paid $9000 a year, and never got a raise. I was asked if I wanted to become a group leader for $10,000. I looked at all the pressure, the chaos, at Tech, and said, "No thanks. Either pay me for all those headaches or just keep me a regular educator."

I believed in the program, what it was doing. We didn't feel valued by the people running it. A few got all the glory. Others were not recognized. Personally I was being fulfilled. Kids came to me flunking and ended up getting C's, B's and even A's.

Stake: Do you mean that happened more than just occasionally? Maybe you just gave them high grades for working hard?

Davis: No, the regular teachers gave the grades. I was just a tutor. Of course I did pick kids I thought I could help.

Stake: You picked out the kids you wanted to work with?

Davis: Sure. Some people went out and got kids they wanted to work with to come into the program. Some would get kids that were poor in attendance, they didn't have bad grades at all. I just looked for kids having trouble in math. Almost all my kids improved their grades. I documented my stuff—for my boss.

HOWARD SAMUELS: Chairman of the board of Cities-in-Schools, New York. Excerpts from an interview, November 1981.

Samuels indicated that the evaluation pointed out what they on the board pretty much knew. The evaluation had failed to show what had been done later to relieve problems in the three targeted cities— and in Houston and Oakland as well.

When asked if there were some problems which first came to the attention of the board because of the evaluation study, Samuels said, "The responsibilities of the evaluation were to indicate the performance of the program in terms of: a) reduced absenteeism; b) improved achievement in school; c) less involvement in juvenile justice systems. . . . Neither the Program's own Management Information System nor the AIR evaluation team kept good enough records on these effects."

Samuels wondered why the evaluation did not give more attention to the integrity of the basic CIS concept, acknowledged by AIR but not really emphasized in the *Final Report*.

Samuels repeatedly indicated that the U.S. society is in trouble because it is not keeping up *productivity*, falling behind in *human capital*, allowing youngsters to remain untrained and uncaring about getting the nation's work done. Much of the fault he attributed to bureaucracies, those in schools as well as in government centers.

He wanted the information to come out in outcome variables (which the evaluators "clearly had promised") so that the people carrying out prime responsibilities—including the national board—could do their jobs. He did not give any indication of support for the evaluation as providing bases for general knowledge on urban education or on services integration.

These comments from people holding various positions in the Cities-in-Schools programs indicate an important disagreement with the evaluation conclusions. They contend that the cultural backgrounds of the evaluators kept them from acknowledging CIS's good work. Key CIS people noted that early evaluation work contributed to program organization. They showed no after-the-fact interest in the extra emphasis given to stakeholders. They were not attentive to the fact that the volume of evaluation data was unexpectedly small. They did not express regret that a major opportunity to increase understanding of social services to urban youth had not apparently proved fruitful. They had a focus. Many felt burned. They believed they had "done right by their kids," but got "no credit from Charlie."

### Karl Kalp and Other Nonprogram Stakeholders

Superintendent Kalp of Indianapolis was pressed by many advocacies. Leaders of the community wanted a special program for estranged youth, but not all wanted this particular program. Some of his staff people had strong notions as to how such a program should be run—and this was not the way. But certain principals were strongly attracted to the Cities-in-Schools approach. At a stakeholder meeting to hear tentative results from Charles Murray, Assistant Superintendent Alexander Moore expressed doubt that the evaluation design (particularly regarding testing and data analysis) had been properly followed.

Eighteen months later, at an interview in the superintendent's office (December 1981), the *Final Report* was discussed. Kalp and curriculum specialist Moore were present, as were assistants William Douglass (federal programs) and William Jones (secondary education). Moore responded to questions put by Deborah Trumbull and me. He implied that he, more than the others, had been responsible locally for monitoring and evaluating the CIS program. He showed no sympathy for it and, again, antipathy for the evaluation project.

When asked about the *Final Report* per se, Karl Kalp did not recall that the district had received any report subsequent to the

*Impact Report* (the one discussed at the heated 30 June 1980 meeting). Moore indicated he knew of the *Final Report* and Douglass in fact had a copy with him. During the meeting of 30 June Charles Murray promised to include a number of missing points in a final report, information that Moore and others had pointed out as needed. Stake asked if these points had been cleared up by the revised *Final Report*. The question was not answered.

Moore expressed surprise that the evaluation reporting at the end was so negative, having felt that previous reports had a tone of CIS advocacy. He and the others did not choose to talk about the *Final Report* content or recommendations, not by refusing to talk about it but by discussing other matters. They were distressed, for example, that Charles Murray had been "defensive" at the stakeholder meeting and that he had not included them in the review-of-draft process for the *Final Report* as he had for the *Impact Report*. Moore said that he could not consider that omission was "accidental"; it troubled him because this was to be a stakeholder evaluation and the district office "had to be considered *the* primary stakeholder" of the Indianapolis Cities-in-Schools project. It appeared that they would not have received a copy of the *Final Report* at all had not CIS City Director William Smith shared a copy with William Douglass, and that was a draft that did not contain the Appendix A reaction statement prepared by the national office of Cities-in-Schools.

When asked whether any of the evaluation findings were of use to the Indianapolis public schools, they seemed to imply that it added nothing new to their understandings. It was seen as troublesome because of its inadequacies as a research piece. The subsequent program (1981) had been scaled to something much smaller, as had the evaluation. There was an interest in continuing what services CIS could provide, but the CIS approach seemed to have nothing special beyond those services—which *could be* delivered in other ways. The central office people were pleased with a shift in emphasis they saw in CIS "away from educational services and toward social services," a recommendation they said they had been making for more than two years.

They were not happy with Murray's implicit recommendation, cited by Stake but not recalled from their reading, that CIS services be redirected at a more willing, less intransigent group of youth, those "with some sort of asset" (p. 110, *Final Report*). A redirection away from those youth appearing to be "sure losers" was contrary to the original purpose, they said. The schools could do a better job of treating those who were willing to try to uplift themselves.

Moore said, "We insisted that CIS declare what it is they are treating." In the spring of 1977, led by Senator Lugar, a common agreement was reached that the CIS goals would be "achievement, attendance, and behavior." This was cited as one instance where the stakeholder approach did something important for the program.

As we left the meeting, I remarked to Deborah Trumbull that it was my perception that the four of them saw no particular merit in the CIS approach and that it should be permitted only so long as it brought in funds that otherwise would not be available. Where best to go from here was not raised once. We went directly to the office of Andrew Paine, the chairman of the Policy Panel, the CIS decision-maker stakeholder group in Indianapolis. His comments follow.

ANDREW PAINE: President, Indiana National Bank; chairman, CIS board, Indianapolis. Also present, his associate, Gregory Lucas, and David Lewis, city CIS director.

Paine: I thought the evaluation was good. I might change some stylistic things . . . use shorter sentences and maybe shorten the report. When I ask experts how to do something, I take their advice. I thought the criticisms of the evaluation were petty. We took the evaluation seriously. Nearly every one of the recommendations in the third report has been implemented (in Indianapolis).

Paine cited factors which he felt led to the initial animosity between CIS and the Indianapolis public schools:

Paine: (1) There was a basic disrespect and fear of Harv Oostdyk. Harv is a committed evangelist, but no manager. He kept changing the program to get more federal money. Harv could not fit into the bureaucratic structure of IPS. The IPS bureaucracy can be described as a perfect bureaucracy . . . there is someone responsible for everything . . . what time of day you're allowed to breathe is discussed at length in policy meeting. And Harv just couldn't fit into that structure . . . this damaged CIS' credibility because people were afraid of Harv. He was thinking light years ahead of where they were operating.

There were rumors of CIS money mismanagement before the CIS policy board got involved.

(2) The IPS resented the fact that CIS could exist separately from the school system and yet have great access to the hierarchical power structure.

(3) There was concern about the exact role of the CIS policy board.

So the picture in Indianapolis was one of clear satisfaction with both CIS and AIR efforts expressed by the spokesperson for the community and of substantial dissatisfaction both with CIS and AIR expressed by the spokesperson for the school district. Termination of federal funding muted the argument. Still, it was an issue to discuss as the district sought a replacement for the retiring superintendent.

The circumstances in Atlanta were somewhat different. There CIS was still active. Atlanta school officials were sympathetic to the evaluators, noting the difficulties they faced.

JARVIS BARNES: Assistant superintendent for research, evaluation, and data processing (also soon to retire), in a conference room near his office on a warm May day in 1982. Also present were Research Associate Myrtice Taylor and Research Assistants Andrew Plankenhorn and Richard Horton. (An earlier portion of the interview appears in mid-Chapter Three).

Barnes: The AIR evaluation study was especially difficult for us. In fact, without question the CIS program was one of the worst designed programs we have encountered. It was very difficult to find out really what the program was. How would they know when it had "done its thing"? There was so much about "process," so much about bringing in community groups, without pinpointing the results. How would you know the good of bringing in these agencies and groups? It got a lot of people from these various agencies and groups, but they did not know how to interact, especially with young people. They could do it one-to-one probably, or in a very unorthodox way. After I saw the way the program was designed I empathized with Murray, and those who were evaluating, because about all they could do was to describe what went on.

The project got started here because of one of two relationships—which you already know. Some local people said, "I wish to hell these people would get out of the way. They are ruining the whole situation. Or I wish they would come in and be a part of it."

Even to this day it is difficult to pinpoint the end product, other than to have a lot of community people coming in, and people bringing groups together. The theory was fine but it was never really operationalized. When you want to apply something as rigorous as statistics to something as loose as that program, it cannot help but be confused.

Stake: But the program people claim they have results, that a large number of young people have been turned around, are starting to reinvest in society.

Barnes: It is a question of cost effectiveness. What are you willing to pay? When are we going to see the results? Five years? Ten years? And by that time how can you pinpoint what really turned them around?

The difficulty in these situations is that you are dealing with human beings and organizations of power. It is so fluid. It's very difficult to maintain a tradition which requires some kind of specification of process.

Plankenhorn: You have to set out some parameters about how the program should be run.

Barnes: Charlie limited his study to Smith High. There they were running a program the way it was supposed to be. Frankly, I could get very little reassurance that they were doing the same thing in St. Luke's or any place else. We have no control over the street academies. They have no commitment to record keeping.

Taylor: No project should be too small to be part of the school system. AIR was not getting data, but we relied on a one-person link without backup. Certain things were not properly administered.

Horton: From CIS objectives we now have an evaluation outline of achievement, attendance, services provided. It measures up pretty well. We are looking at changes in pre and post scores.

Barnes: The project is hesitant to use these variables as critical. It is very humanistic.

Stake: Have you made use of the AIR *Final Report*?

Barnes: No, I have not had occasion to use it, but it is more the jurisdiction of the Area and Program people (curriculum, counseling).

At Arsenal Technical High School in Indianapolis in December 1981, Deborah Trumbull and I chatted with Cynthia, Chris, and Larry, all students who had been in the CIS program for at least two years.

Cynthia said: "My CIS counselor cares about me . . . the teacher sometimes don't pay attention to me. In CIS I learned that I have to listen . . . sometimes I have a problem listening to what the teacher says." Chris talked about the tickets he received to the Pacers' basketball games. He also mentioned some CIS tutoring he received when he was having math problems. Larry spoke about a problem with an art teacher because he "mouthed off." He talked it over with his counselor, who suggested better ways of dealing with his art teacher. "Now we get along fine."

The students said they liked Arsenal Tech: "Over at the other school, they've had three or four riots this year." None of them seemed aware of CIS as a social services reform effort, or the evaluation of it.

Trumbull and I checked further on the "outstationing" of Indianapolis agency personnel.

ELLEN ANNALA: Assistant director of the Near East Side Multi-Service Center, 1977–80. She had been responsible for hiring and providing on-going training for all the Near East staff working with CIS.

She expressed concern that CIS staff people had often not been qualified. She saw the coordinated services within Cities-in-Schools difficult to manage because of the complex management design. "No one could ever draw me a structural chart," she said. She mentioned difficulties with funding and a lack of accountability of her center's CIS workers, difficulties aggravated by different job locations.

In New York City on two occasions I talked with Paula Lipsitz.

PAULA LIPSITZ: Agency Liaison Program Coordinator, Community Board Assistance Unit, Mayor's Office, City of New York.

From an interview in July 1980 I learned that at that time Paula Lipsitz had the responsibility of keeping the mayor's office informed about social service efforts in various communities within the city. She was particularly interested in and perplexed by efforts to coordinate the welfare and education efforts. She claimed to like the ideas of CIS but had learned little from it about how to organize and manage individual sites. Lipsitz said she had not been attentive to the internal management of CIS. She had not read the AIR evaluation reports, nor had she expected them to be useful to her problems. She was satisfied that the social service coordinations of CIS are worthwhile and believed that the evaluation should indicate what minimum arrangements might accomplish them.

One of the most valuable sources of information about the AIR evaluation work was:

HELEN BRANCH: Area III Instructional Resource Person, Atlanta public schools.

Until 1981 she held a liaison responsibility with the evaluators. She found large communication problems among program evaluation and stakeholder people. The following are excerpts from her letter to me, dated January 1981.

In the case of Cities-in-Schools in Atlanta, there was, in my opinion, not enough direct contact between evaluators and stakeholders to develop the kind of communication needed. Certainly there was not a "solicitous and friendly" relationship as someone (at the ERS annual meeting) in Arlington suggested. More likely the relationship could be called "hostile" on several occasions. Generally, the final outcome is friendly, but I suspect it is because the project staff is relieved because they feel that the *Final Report* will not paint as bleak a picture as they previously thought it would.

Regarding the function of AIR as evaluators, I want to say that they started out great. They were punctual, compassionate but assertive, and thorough in planning and communication. However, as time went on and personnel changes were frequent, they lapsed into a more "traditional" function. That is, they wanted the "hard data" and spent not enough of the right kind of effort to get the "soft data." In their defense, they did have personnel problems at the local site that are difficult to deal with from Washington. I put considerable effort into assisting with those local problems so I know the size of the obstacle. Furthermore, the Atlanta Public Schools Computer Center had difficulty in processing the "hard data" for AIR (as per agreement with the NIE contracted in 1977 and renewed each year). I do not know how other evaluation contractors handle such problems, but I can see that there were many things that got in the way of a good evaluation. I had experienced many of the same difficulties in doing the evaluations of Project Propinquity for three years before it became the Cities-in-Schools project.

Through my nine years of work in the Research and Evaluation division of Atlanta Public Schools, I experienced and observed a gradual decline in enthusiasm, and increased cynical attitude toward evaluation of social and educational programs. There are so many problems ranging from those associated with intractable bureaucracies to those related to the tenacity with which many people cling to their self-destructive ways of living.

None of these civil servants were able to indicate that the evaluation findings were useful. Nor had they high expectations. They recognized many of the political obstacles to learning what might work and were not surprised that the evaluation study had so little to say.

Stanley Stern: Vice-president, Mid-west National Bank.

Stern was an Indianapolis stakeholder of note and spoke as such at the annual meeting of the Evaluation Research Society in Arlington in 1980. He spoke heartily of his city's need to make youth productive citizens and part of the work force. He told of the Lilly Foundation's support of Oostdyke and Milliken and how support for a major effort of CIS in Indianapolis haltingly occurred. He noted that no evaluation would be acceptable and useful to all stakeholders. The "sophisticated" AIR evaluation was attractive to business people but not to school district people, "who attacked it with petty criticism." He concluded with observations that CIS people "have something good" and that the Indianapolis policy group (decision-maker stakeholders) had welded it together.

HENRY ZIMMER: United Way director of planning and government relations, Atlanta. Excerpts from written correspondence, December 1980.

According to Zimmer, officials of United Way had been routinely questioning continued support of Cities-in-Schools, more particularly Carver High School's Project Propinquity. Barbara Cleveland, a free-lance consultant, was commissioned to do a brief evaluation study. The AIR *Final Report* was just being drafted, but it was recognized that Carver was not getting AIR attention to the extent desired.[2] Henry Zimmer had attended three stakeholder meetings set up by AIR and had been somewhat discouraged by the slowness of CIS development and AIR's inability to answer certain questions. He arranged Cleveland's assignment.

Cleveland interviewed people from the schools, Cities-in-Schools, and four agencies: the Fulton County Department of Family and Children Services, the city's Youth Development Division, and the Metropolitan Atlanta Boys' Club and Girls' Club. She reviewed reports and files. She organized her study around issues of program operations and of interagency relationships.

Noting, as had Charles Murray, that Carver kept CIS students in *regular* classes throughout the day, making CIS there an after-school activity, she wrote: "This complete absence of regular, intensive contacts with the CIS students makes the development of "close, personal" relationships almost impossible, especially considering the physical extent of the school's campus and the size of each CIS caseload" (p. 3).

A list of such organizational problems were detailed. Personnel and jurisdictional problems were mentioned. These findings were not dissimilar to those of the AIR study, though the implication of "territorial" dispute was stronger in Cleveland's report. (She had the

---

2. It seems that a stakeholder evaluation such as AIR's, even though it aimed for a "national" audience, should have been able to provide answers to stakeholder Henry Zimmer's questions. It is reasonable, of course, for any official to seek a "second opinion," so the commissioning should not be seen particularly as stemming from disappointment in the AIR work.

advantage of quickly getting in and out, not needing to preserve rapport and access.)

NORMAN GOLD: Developer of the stakeholder evaluation design and here the evaluation program monitor, thus a stakeholder in this evaluation contract. He was the federal person who became most acquainted with Cities-in-Schools. He held the title of Senior Research Associate for Evaluation, NIE.

In an article in *Education Times* (3 November 1980), Gold was quoted: "Whenever possible, we should use observed behavior rather than standardized tests." Also: "People must either adjust their expectations or accept urban intervention programs as failure. The cost-benefit mentality keeps pushing evaluation into generalizations that neither help the educational process nor correctly measure reality."

In a phone conversation with me on 11 March 1982 Gold said:

There was no great expectation, in NIE, that CIS would contribute much.

In doing this evaluation we could have searched out all the variant forms of Cities-in-Schools. We chose an elaborate look at the process and impact of the "pure form." Our resources were spread thin. We were ambitious. We had to narrow down though, especially with Harv running around creating new things. Someone had to create some stability. We decided to confine ourselves to CIS "pure form," which appeared to us to be, among other things, the most stable. Of course, we hoped we would be able to discuss some of the new variants.

There was good reason to get the Technical Review Panel together. In a sense they were technology stakeholders, but they were there to validate the evaluation study, not to run the study. They made useful comments. The big difficulty was that they wanted to do a research study rather than an applied evaluation study. Without them we were not monitoring the technical quality of the work. It was more complicated than any one mind could do.

Gold's research group leader was Charles Stalford. In May 1980, after reading a draft of this metaevaluation review, Stalford wrote me:

NIE's Division of Testing, Assessment and Evaluation did take steps to gain broader use of the urban education information we were gaining from CIS and other programs. A May 1980 conference was initiated, chaired by Norm, "Start-up and Implement Considerations in School Based Intervention Programs."

At that same time there was a short-lived "youth initiative" proposed by the Carter administration. We engaged in conversation with Bob Schwartz, an NIE staff member who was coordinating the educational segment of planning for the initiative. The fact that there was an election and a change of administration in Washington with significant consequences for the whole philosophy of programming (i.e., block grants versus categorical programs) as well as different substantive emphases, in my judgment, cannot be over-estimated as a determinant of the ultimate use of CIS.

At my suggestion, Norm edited the papers from the 1980 conference into a proceedings document. It is now substantially ready for publication, but has not been published because of a government-wide moratorium on such printing.

KATHLYN MOSES: Director of the Office of Urban Initiatives, U.S. Department of Education.

Kathlyn was responsible for coordinating the federal support for CIS. She appeared at a number of stakeholder meetings and kept a lively interest in the progress of the evaluation work. In an interview with me in November 1981 she summarized her views of that work:

I question the evaluation of many inner city demonstration projects. Most of the programs administered out of this office deal more with changes in behavioral patterns. In any evaluation, that would be our first attack, then we would look at achievement scores. I'm quite sure that the AIR evaluation took that approach.

From talking with students when we were monitoring the site, I do think benefits occurred. We can't get at this through achievement scores and achievement records. Of course, if we can't measure this behavior, then we can't use hard data. The sites themselves are so uneven in their stages of development and in their process of delivering services that a blanket statement talking about all of Cities-in-Schools is not quite fair.

Evaluation is absolutely necessary for the planning, development and growth of a program But evaluation should be used in a positive way and not a negative way. We shouldn't use evaluation to punish people. We should use evaluation to help them. And eventually we must use measurements. We're in school for one purpose, and that's for learning. We've got to measure the achievement along the way. We aren't a community service. We're in education. Education is the business of learning. We've got to measure that achievement.

The Department of Education and NIE worked so closely with the AIR study. I doubt that the findings would have been different had the Office of Education undertaken the study alone.

I have used the AIR report a great deal. I've used the last chapter on recommendations. I have used the findings. I did not pay much attention to the statistics. I was not really convinced how accurate those statistics were.

I have used the first chapter dealing with the history. I've used the report in working with the project directors and when I make on-site visits. I think there were some very solid recommendations.

I can't think of any other federal officials who have paid attention to the *Final Report*. We did a summary, in this office, and sent it up the ladder. If anyone read it, I don't know. I've received no comments.

The report was used recently in a meeting with members of the Health, Education, and Labor Committee when they were discussing programs in urban areas. I guess we can use the report more for public relations than anything else.

On these previous pages I have presented testimony of a number of stakeholders about the integrity and usefulness of the evaluation of Cities-in-Schools. These excerpts and summaries were taken from longer exchanges which in full reflect a feeling that AIR had not enlightened them very much—neither generally about urban education nor about the particular effects individual projects and case workers were having. Several pointed out, as is indicated in the paragraphs above, that the evaluation report was useful in certain political ways.

### Robert Perloff and Other Technical Review Panelists

Robert Perloff was chair of the Technical Review Panel. He chose to act as facilitator of review and moderator at meetings rather than as a reviewer himself. He performed this function well.

MALCOLM KLEIN: sociologist, specialist in juvenile systems, University of Southern California.

In September 1981 the Technical Review Panel gathered in L.A. for a final time, taking a retrospective look at CIS, AIR, and at its own performance. As one of the panel members, Klein presented four criticisms of Murray's evaluation work, as indicated in the following excerpts:

At the very first meeting of the Technical Review Panel, we spent a lot of time talking about messianic leadership associated with this program. We were concerned how the evaluation was going to take account of that. It seems to me it's worthwhile documenting and worthwhile understanding the chances of institutionalization and implementation given this form of leadership.

My second question is, How do the Plan B's of the world evolve? Does a

Plan B evolve with alternative rationales involving alternative operations or do alternative operations develop and then alternative rationales are used to justify these after the fact? You have a beautiful example here of a Plan B evolving and I'm not sure, Charlie, that you've made as much of this as you could have.

My third point has to do with evaluating caseworker impacts. The report spends some time on the impact of the caseworkers but there's no comparative base. We don't know what other kinds of workers could have done. The description of the caseworker failures to contact the names and get involved in the lives of the kids and so forth is interesting, but I don't know if that is special in any way.

CIS did get off the hook in Chapter 4. I've been waiting, with prejudice, to see the case studies. I was against that approach. Now I've seen the cases. I find them terribly disappointing. They are not, to me, case studies at all. They are little vignettes and anecdotes about particular kids. The case studies are superficial and demonstrate nothing more than the selection of anecdotes.

I get so damn angry reading the appendix pages. It's so typical, the attempt of program administrators to get off the hook by using pseudo data or inappropriate data to show how they got off the hook. It's chock full of errors and it's going to negate half of the impact that your report can have.

Throughout the study, Klein had tried to maximize the value of the evaluation research to the public policy community, urging the evaluators to demand more conformance of the CIS people to original plans. He offered many suggestions as to how this research could tie into other studies of the juvenile justice system. He was not unaware of the tentativeness of data gathering in these circumstances, but expressed dismay that Charles Murray had not "made as much of this study" as he could have.

WARD EDWARDS: Director, Social Science Research Institute, University of Southern California.

Here are excerpts from written correspondence from Edwards, another panelist, to Charles Murray in 1981, in response to draft materials distributed to the Technical Review Panel:

For myself, I think the major thing I learned from reading the AIR document was the evaluations should be commissioned in the formative phases of programs, not because the programs themselves should be evaluated so soon but because the incidental benefits to the program are great, and are probably attainable in no other way.

The *Final Report* has a major problem. That problem is that in the course of a multi-year evaluation, the evaluators get so close to both program ideas and program people that they lose perspective (or in this case, while not losing perspective they come to wish they could), see too many specific trees in addition to the forest, and end up with a "bottom line" that reflects the wishful thinking of the evaluation. It is not my intent to argue that the wishful thinking of the program people does not belong to the evaluation document—it does. But it should not be presented as the bottom line of the evaluation, and in this case it almost is.

Nowhere does the report discuss what seems to me to be the real problem: how to take the core of good ideas that lie in the CIS concept as evaluated and implement them within an existing power structure. The CIS leaders at the national level have been very clever about doing so—but that kind of creative leadership lasts for a while, and then wanes and is gone.

Moreover, such leaders are much better for setting up demonstrations than they are for dealing with the true problem—after all, this whole national-scale evaluation is looking at results for three schools. Money and power lie at the core of ghetto problems—as they do at the core of most others. Yet the discussion of both is brief and unsuggestive about the future.

You conclude that the kids did, in general, have major problems. Would that conclusion have been appropriate for any random sample from the student population of the same school? I assume you have that information; at least the statistically competent among your readers will want to know it. You kept giving reports of U.S. conditions and consequences, without ever giving comparison information. You must have it. I'm not asking for tests of significance—I know better. I am asking for some $2 \times 2$ tables. Or if I can't have that, please give me at least some reason to believe that what you are telling me does not characterize the school population in general. If you expect academics to need and respect this evaluation report, you cannot afford not to respond to this. It will hamper readability for others, so you may want to do something clever with appendices. But something must be done.

The scientific message will surely be lost, if you leave things as they are. The interpretation you will get is "Charlie likes the CIS people and the CIS concept, and defended both with consummate skill; the only trouble is, his data don't support his argument."

Edwards' advice to Murray was quite in contrast to Klein's. Edwards believed in formal presentations of options but adaptive research (formative evaluation) operations. He too mentioned omitted issues, particularly regarding development of new sites. Still, he indicated that Murray had done about as good a job as one could under the circumstances.

EDYS QUELLMALZ: An educational evaluator from UCLA.

Quellmalz joined the panel at the very end; here are excerpts from her remarks at the September 1981 meeting:

In my opinion, one lesson we have learned from the CIS experience is that federal "seed" money [should] be more judiciously allocated. I would recommend reconsideration of the features that constitute a describably, replicable prototype and opt, initially, for a smaller-scale on-site, short-term funding strategy. It should be acknowledged as a development venture with formative evaluation as an integral component of the development process. If the program doesn't even work on one site, then funding prototypes, development and more formal evaluations in additional sites would not be warranted.

One problem I have with the *Final Report* is the insularity of the evaluation. The report alludes to "other" demonstration programs and their complex varying structures. How were their features similar or different from those of CIS? What methodological problems encountered in the CIS evaluations have occurred in evaluations of other social service programs? We get the impression that when CIS was implemented in its "pure" form (in Indianapolis, 1978–79) it worked pretty well "for a social intervention program." What does that mean? What indicators are used in other social action research to demonstrate effectiveness or progress? The report leaves me feeling that I need a larger frame of reference.

One of the problems I had with the evaluation report concerns how does the methodology in this evaluation relate to the types of methodologies that have been used for other social action programs? People on the Technical Review Panel could have helped with this information.

I was most troubled by the evaluation's measures of educational impact. Standardized test scores and course grades are often quite insensitive to the specific instructional foci of the program, let alone the individualized tutoring sessions. Often program personnel are distressed when they see progress in achievement and work habits, but global measures don't credit the change and improvement. The evaluation might have used: (1) criterion-referenced test performance carefully matched to objectives taught in CIS classes and remedial reading sessions; (2) records of assignments turned in and completed; and (3) counts of problems or questions successfully completed. Just as student self concept, attitudes and other behaviors might improve in small ways, a more detailed collection of work samples, instructor observations and evaluator observations might have provided more and better information about academic progress. Both CIS program staff and the evaluators seemed to feel that CIS classes (some at least) did make a difference. On what, how?

I would recommend that evaluations of diffuse programs with an educational component include measures of achievement, attitude and effort carefully matched to what specifically is taught. When observations and staff comments indicate that they see progress, the evaluation can attempt to find a systematic way to describe and measure it.

Quellmalz emphasized the need for good outcome data. So had most review panelists all along. AIR's rationale was similar to

Quellmalz's. Murray had worked strenuously to have exactly that, but at study's end he had small cell frequencies and challenged instrumentation. How he could have gotten a respectable collection of data is not clear. The social scientists here, Murray, Quellmalz, and others insisted on common, relevant measures of change for large numbers of students. It is not clear that such data could have been obtained. The advisors seldom discussed the likelihood that their advice could be followed. William Cooley (last excerpt to follow) did.

LEE SECHREST: Director of the Center for Research of Scientific Knowledge, University of Michigan.

Sechrest was present at only the last two meetings. In September 1981, in response to a draft of the *Final Report*, he wrote to Charles Murray and Robert Perloff.

In general I think that the report is quite fair to CIS and that at the same time it presents a reasonable picture from which decision makers might approach the development of similar programs should they desire to do so. The tone of the presentation is judicious throughout being tinged both with the objectivity that one expects from scientists and the sympathy that one is likely to have for well meaning program specialists operating under exceedingly difficult conditions.

In my view the conclusions presented in the fourth volume of the report are generally supportable and warranted. They are if anything, slightly more favorable toward CIS than they might have been in other hands. I think the report may be slightly kinder toward CIS in relation to the matter of accomplishing intermediate goals than I would be inclined to be. The report, it seems to me, comes close to implying that if a program is able to accomplish its intermediate goals and fails to have any impact because of the broader social consensus in which it operates then the program may in some manner be construed as having some value. In my view the external social circumstances are part of the legitimate context for planning programs and if those circumstances do not permit the realization of the longer term desired outcomes then the accomplishment of the intermediate goal is of no consequence.

I also think that the report implies in one or two places that rather more is known about CIS than was actually established. A notable instance is on page 114 where it is stated that "CIS demonstrated its capacity to develop these relationships with students who are believed to be the most difficult to reach." The problem is with the rather positive verb "demonstrated." In conjunction with the term "capacity" all in all the statement is quite positive. In fact, in my estimation the data show only that under some otherwise unspecifiable circumstances relationships with students do develop. The statement as it stands rather implies, it seems to me, that CIS can go out and develop these relationships upon command. Certainly, that was never demonstrated. Nonetheless, despite my minor objections I am satisfied with the conclusions of the report.

There should be some way in which program evaluation could come to be seen as an important function in program building in more positive efforts to achieve effective social interventions. I do not necessarily mean by this any simple minded notions about formative evaluation and telling people how to improve programs. Instead, it seems to me, that something considerably more fundamental must be undertaken. I wonder, for example, whether ERS might take a more public and vigorous stance concerning the need for long term funding of program development activities and move away from seeming advocacy of one-shot summative evaluations. The program has been poorly and uncertainly funded with no assurances that it would be around for any considerable length of time in order for needed program development work to take place. I am not sure what ERS might do in order to promote these longer run and future oriented program development activities but I am quite persuaded that we are not going to make progress we desire in solving important social programs until we have the opportunity to develop and exploit longer range perspectives.

In respect to a lot of social programs, somehow or other, people do not take social science seriously in the way they take other sciences seriously.

I think we'll never come close to resolving or solving a lot of issues and problems until we can get people to take (their own plans) seriously and follow them. CIS is a good example, it was never followed.

PETER ROSSI: University of Massachusetts, was originally invited to be a member of the panel but never made it to a meeting. At study's end he was president of the American Sociological Association.

At the Evaluation Research Society meeting in 1980, Rossi said that his one reservation about the AIR evaluation was that it seemed to "ooze TLC" (tender loving care), with of course the possible price to be paid, "going native" (co-option). He felt that Murray might be leaning over backward to soften the blow. "Apparently," he said, "the project never got implemented." It provided "a few superficial friends to kids." The evaluation report is successful in saying that there is not much of a program there, providing little other than a personal touch. The program rhetoric promises much more.

WILLIAM COOLEY: Education psychologist, University of Pittsburgh. He was president of the American Educational Research Association.

At the 1980 Evaluation Research Society session Cooley, still another latecomer panelist, objected to broadening the concept "client" to "stakeholder," and thus diversifying and confusing the attention being paid to impact analysis. It would be enough for an evaluation study such as this to tell accurately and in depth (a) who is being served; (b) what is it they are receiving; and (c) how much it is costing. "Good answers to these questions," he said, "will better inform those who have responsibility for 'impact' than will direct measurement of impact."

During the Technical Review Panel Meeting, 1981, Cooley said (excerpted):

We all know that there are three kinds of activity going on in the name of impact assessment. The experimenters insist that the only way you can do it is through experimental design. I think most of us recognize that it is seldom possible to do this. At least that's the conclusion that I've come to in the education context. Then there are the modelers. Their solution is to specify the model for the outcome, develop structural equations and test them. Then there are the process describers. Their way to make convincing statements about program impact is to get good descriptions of what is happening in the program. As I've worked in evaluation it is the latter I've found to be the most convincing. According to my recent experience, the most convincing impact statements are based on good process description. Most clients I deal with agree.

I've spent many years worrying about how to assess impact quantitatively. I'm very sympathetic to the approach. I've looked at a lot of data in ways that allow me to change the statistical model and see how dramatically different my impact statement might be. I think we have oversold our ability to make program impact statements quantitatively. I really don't feel that you can make impact statements quantitatively, given the state of our knowledge in this CIS type of study.

There are a lot of necessary conditions for valid quantitative demonstrations of program impact. When those conditions aren't present and a client still wants insight into program impact, what we can do is make good process descriptions. In the cities many agencies are out there to help poor kids. They are running into each other, instead of consolidating their efforts. So, good descriptions of how they are running into each other without CIS, and how they are coming together with CIS, would be very convincing information about the impact CIS is having.

As from the beginning, these several members of the Technical Review Panel were concerned about the integrity of the evaluation work. Over several years they had urged a highly rigorous design and carefully developed instruments. They approached their task with different views as to what research should accomplish and had different notions as to what this research did accomplish. The panelists tried to be supportive of Murray. At the final meetings it was easiest to blame the program, as Murray did, for not operating according to plan and for keeping inadequate records. Only William Cooley seemed to express real doubt that evaluation research, as planned by AIR with help from ERS panelists, even if fully carried out, *could* provide information useful to those responsible for the social rehabilitation of outcast urban youth.

# 5

## The Evaluators' Accomplishment

The troubling hypothesis represented by the title *Quieting Reform* is that this AIR research activity muted the services to youngsters— not only to the evaluated youth in Atlanta, Indianapolis, and New York City but to all urban youth. After an epistemological look at the knowledge AIR "produced" and after a practical look at the utility of the study to stakeholders, the effect of such research on efforts to reform social services will be discussed.

The Cities-in-Schools program brought together three propitious ideas: (1) personalization of human services, (2) integration of community agency service, and (3) ameliorative adult-youth interaction at school sites largely in the form of schoolwork. The *Final Report* indicated that CIS caseworkers were often able to establish rapport and to engage large numbers of youngsters in desirable activities. Relying heavily on political luminaries and corporate leaders for support, CIS nevertheless failed to gain substantial support from those more directly in charge of community agencies and schools. The program itself remained a possession of founders Harold Oostdyk, William Milliken, and associates. It did not draw the schools or agencies into vital partnerships. Nor did CIS achieve the officially designated intermediate goals for youth, i.e., aggregate improvements in attendance and scholastic achievement and reduction of juvenile delinquency.

A fact most obvious to the evaluators was that good data were extremely difficult to obtain. This was attributed in large part to poor project management in each of the three cities and at the na-

129

tional level. There was a shortage of good case records, partly because the projects were not well organized. The evaluators at first blamed the poor organization on three factors: the inexperience of the founders, sudden expansions in program activity, and the "personalism" ethic (which encouraged caseworkers and projects to be individualistic). But in the end Charles Murray blamed even more the diverse requirements of separate funding sources, particularly the seven federal agencies. *One principal AIR conclusion was that efforts to redirect the most wayward urban youth should await major reconceptualization of the federal role in welfare—a timely theme with the new Reagan-appointed department heads.*

Encouraged collectively by NIE personnel, evaluation colleagues, and school officials—and loyal to the legacy of AIR's historic Project Talent—the evaluation team remained committed to a quantitative test of impact. Charles Murray had a rationale for studying "process"—for helping the project build better solutions—but the investigative energies of his research here were devoted to determining the outcomes of a treatment. Conceptually, the "treatment" was a generic form of Cities-in-Schools. This was to be a social science study featuring statistical analysis of aggregate scores to provide generalizations about social services delivery. Murray provided early formative assistance to projects so as to maximize the likelihood that such a test could occur. When it became apparent the data base would be too weak for such an analysis, individual student records were searched to determine the "best case" the program might make. Finding records for "the most helped youngsters" to be incomplete and problematic, Murray concluded that substantial gains had not occurred, certainly not an impact worthy of the federal investment of $10 million.

Cities-in-Schools did not deliver on many of its promises. No one disputes that. It did deliver something. Just what it did deliver remains in doubt. Even though AIR rhetoric emphasized the need for measuring incremental growth, these evaluators did not set their micrometers to just barely noticeable differences or to individualistic turnaround. Generally, AIR relied on measurements (i.e., observation and records) made by others: district test people, CIS evaluators, caseworkers, teachers. Those records indeed were not good enough. Clearly the data were incomplete. Apparently CIS caseworkers did not overstate progress, as might be expected if there were apprehension about the evaluation. They may have understated it. It has been suggested that some caseworkers distrusted the evaluators and did not cooperate with them. No one suggested there was widespread gain on the designated criterion variables that AIR failed to see, but program people cited instance after instance of good work, implying that AIR did not use its expertise to document the help CIS did provide.

Charles Murray wanted to carry out what AIR had promised. But he did not analyze CIS program outcomes as promised partly because CIS did not provide the program promised. Furthermore, school district officials did not provide data they had contracted to provide. Consequently, AIR reports described the projects in detail and arrived at a largely indisputable conclusion: "CIS impact was imperceptible." Could more have been expected of AIR? Yes.

The evaluation study was not as fair as it could have been to the CIS program and to protagonistic parents and youngsters. AIR people did not adequately inform CIS people that AIR's primary interest was in gathering information useful for guiding national development of CIS-like programs rather than on identification of local accomplishment. AIR evaluators did not organize their research to study cases or team processes. There was little formal observation of what was happening, and not happening, to these youngsters. The evidence Murray found was sufficient to justify the conclusion that what was promised to funders was not delivered. CIS students were not making what most readers would consider an "investment in society." But Murray responded only a little to program claims of widespread assistance, provision of good adult role-models, diminution of hostility, increased awareness of predicament, and more. Murray repeatedly asked CIS people to identify criteria by which CIS might better be assessed. They did not, possibly could not. But criterion identification is the expected forte of evaluators, not necessarily of paraprofessional social workers. CIS's inability to describe program quality did not justify so meager a search.

Even though CIS was a costly program, some would argue that the federal effort did not represent more than a fair share of the common wealth due those underprivileged youth. CIS advocates reminded us of a societal obligation to try to relieve conditions of impoverishment even when we do not know how much we will accomplish. They urged us to base evaluation more on whether their program is the most logical and compassionate of alternatives available, less on whether their program is the most efficient or effective.

Logic and compassion are not the usual criteria for formal assessment of government programs, but they too are defensible criteria. Furthermore, the usual criteria often lead us toward a "cease and desist" conclusion. Program opponents interpret *"No significant gains were observed"* to mean that *"No assistance is justified at this time."* Of course that is a misinterpretation of the finding, but if research is regularly misinterpreted in a way that deprives certain citizens of equity, then even well-reasoned criteria need to be reconsidered.

AIR began by looking for what CIS would surely do, and ended by finding what CIS had not done. A better description of what CIS was and what it actually did would have served some stakeholders better. It is unlikely but possible that if stakeholders knew what actually was accomplished, they would have judged it a successful program even if it did not fulfill grand intentions.[1]

Had AIR enthusiastically taken this more descriptive approach it would have been in trouble, opposed by most government officials, most program evaluation specialists, and most funding agency rep-

---

1. Reviewers of manuscript drafts have urged me to indicate more directly how *I* might have done this evaluation study. I fear that already I am drawing too much attention to my evaluation ideas at the expense of attention to those of Charles Murray, Norman Gold, and the ERS panelists. But it may be important here to say that in much evaluation research I personally find decision maker stakeholder values given too much emphasis, consumer stakeholder values too little. Even with my strong ideology I am displeased to see evaluation research driven by ideological purpose, including that great good aim: to reform governance. Evaluation studies usually should illuminate the activity at hand, engage ideological as well as practical issues, and indicate merit and shortcoming. I admire disciplined study and precision of measurement, yet oppose fixed designs insensitive to context, emerging issue, and program change. Evaluations are political, and equity is a consideration in design as well as in interpretation. Neither rigor nor empathy nor completeness nor clarity is virtuous beyond cost; each is part of trade-offs that the evaluator must resolve.

In this CIS case I would have sought a rich, balanced, frank description with less attention to uniform measurement of attendance, achievement, and trouble with police. I would have tried to study operator and consumer stakeholder issues more, some even though not hearing them voiced. I would not limit my attention to those issues, or try to present them in a way to advance their cause, or give "affirmative action" because they usually are undervalued. My conclusions as to program effect would probably have been the same as Murray's, but my description and implication of program worth would have ranged further.

resentatives. Many evaluators are sympathetic to the arguments for
formative evaluation rather than summative, for the productivity of
process-establishment rather than a productivity defined by in-
tended-impact. Evaluators faced vexed critics, many not compre-
hending the limitations of impact analysis. If there was serious fault
with AIR design, if it should have abandoned the hypothesis-testing
approach sooner, the fault rests more with those who commissioned
and sustained the faulty design. It is they who were the key *evaluation* stakeholders (as distinct from program stakeholders). They insisted on a rigorous test of the impact of CIS services integration.
Many of them were personally identified and committed to "social
science as quantification." In no small way they are responsible for
the insufficiency of information about what Cities-in-Schools accomplished in three cities in 1978, 1979, and 1980.

Social science methods can be used to describe a complex array
of actual accomplishments—but if used merely to find statistically
significant differences or covariates, the result will be simplistic. An
alternative design is needed. Evaluation specialists often debate the
advantages of quantitative versus qualitative methods, but too seldom debate the utility of generalistic versus particularist evaluation designs—and implications for social reform.

### The Production of Knowledge

The evaluation study was created by NIE to see if the *CIS idea*
had merit. It was expected that project activities would be scru-
tinized at several sites in each of the three cities not so much to
learn the good they would do for Atlanta, New York, and Indianapolis
youngsters, but to learn whether CIS, as a general approach, could
be counted on to do a better job of services integration and personal
support to troubled and troublesome youth—at existing funding levels. As I said in the opening paragraph of this review, NIE and AIR
were seeking policy-relevant generalizations for program administrators in cities, school districts, and funding agencies across the
country.

Research methods can be sorted into two classes of inquiry. Designers of evaluation studies can design their inquiries (1) with
relatively greater emphasis on producing statements of general relationship (among prominent elements or constructs) or (2) with
relatively greater emphasis on producing descriptions of particular

events (and their contingencies and contextuality). It is a choice between *generalization* and *particularization*.[2]

The first way, sometimes called the scientific,[3] the positivistic,
the formalistic, or the rational approach, is preferred by most social
scientists. They are seeking parsimonious, context-free, universal
explanations, hopefully relevant in all situations though perhaps
not revealing the determining influence in most. This approach usually makes its way to grand generalization by deliberate selection
of a few key variables, careful identification of populations and
samples, and analysis of measurements for large numbers of cases.

Disciplined researchers who follow the established procedures
create new knowledge, new generalizations. They indicate tenden-
cies to be expected in large numbers of subsequent observations.
Just what will happen in the next single instance is of course not
determined, but the chances are sometimes improved that the outcome will be predicted. Social science generalizations might indicate, for example, that charismatic leaders tend to create organizations which set unattainable goals for individual members. Whether
or not that would pertain to the next Cities-in-Schools project of
course is not thus determined, even if it were a sound generalization, for with social phenomena the descriptors are tenuous and ex-
ceptions to the rule are common. But with suitable cautions, the
generalizations may improve program management.

The second way of designing evaluation studies, sometimes
called the naturalistic, the phenomenological, the clinical, or the intuitive, is common in life's ordinary problem solving. Being more
subjective, this way is considered suspect by many social scientists.
Its advocates are often professional persons faced with problem situations, *each* of which has an essential importance. These practitioners seek historical, contextual, "personalistic" understandings,

---

2. In *The Reflective Practitioner* Donald Schön wrote of these options as
a choice between rigor and relevance (p. 42, 1982). Fine reviews of these alternatives have been published by Georg Von Wright (1971) and David
Hamilton (1977).The alternatives are prominent in the literature on philosophy of social science.

3. "Scientific" need not mean formalistic, analytic, quantitative, standardized, and grandly generalized. Science is any orderly, dispassionate
quest for understanding. But those who have striven to make their research
"more scientific" and their science more rigorous usually have emphasized
these five characteristics.

hopefully relevant for the individual case whether or not a basis for understanding large numbers of cases. This approach makes its way toward conditional or limited generalization by: labored identification of critical moments or symptoms, attention to patterns of covariation within the context, recognition of classic examples, and careful exploration of the uniqueness of the situation. A case study may be prepared.

Highly experienced researchers who rely on this approach create new knowledge, new generalizations, but generalizations having narrower limits, situational constraints. These researchers recognize an immediate case's membership in a class or population of cases and may provide additional acquaintance with other members of the group. Just what will happen in the very next situation is of course not determined, but if the vicarious experience or typologizing is good, chances are sometimes improved that the next case will be better managed, or at least better understood.

The evaluation specialist may describe the activities and problems of an organization, noting the events, valuings, personalities— all in context. To again cite the example, program leadership might be charismatic and the member goals unattainable, but more additional information would be seen as pertinent. Whether or not this would aid preparations for a new Cities-in-Schools project is not assured, but knowledge of what seemed to work and not to work this one time might enrich the experience of the new managers to some extent and increase the chances of success. Many managers believe it does.

For the development of education and social institutions, which kind of knowledge will be more useful: grand generalizations or particularistic knowledge? Both are needed. But certain users or situations call for one kind more than the other. Evaluation specialists designing program evaluation studies expect to provide some of each. But because different specialists have different questions and different audiences and because the two approaches call for rather different allocation of resources, designers usually choose to emphasize one kind over the other.

In the case of Cities-in-Schools, support for just a small portion of the nation's urban youth was very expensive. It could be justified perhaps only if it could be said to be a "demonstration project"— developing knowledge or experience that would pay off in many other cities. Production of knowledge was a common responsibility of the CIS program and the AIR evaluation. The *general* idea of CIS needed to be tested.

Most scientists in AIR, NIE, and the Evaluation Research Society have a strong preference for the formalistic approach. The design had to be respectable in their eyes or it would not have been accepted.[4] Charles Murray preferred the formalistic approach. Not more than three members of his Technical Review Panel expressed doubt; one noted that AIR risked committing the entire budget to a few generalizations that might somehow turn out to be obscure or trivial. Murray was confident his previous field experience would draw him into adequate attention to contextual detail and that the national value of CIS would be better demonstrated in the formalistic ways suggested in the proposal.

"Knowledge production" (to use bureaucratic jargon) can be measured much more easily when it is formal, e.g., in written or symbolic form, than when it is formed by readers in their own minds from descriptive accounts. When social scientists talk about knowledge production, they are usually talking about generalizations written for widespread distribution and policy making. The attention in the remainder of this section will be on formal knowledge produced, with personal knowledge to be considered later in the section on utility of the study.

### Problem Reduction vs. Solution Building

In his summary Chapter IV, "The Potential of CIS," Charles Murray made a substantial effort to provide generalizable knowledge. Much of it was negative. He opened the chapter with this brief summary of "lessons learned."

We have learned that a program which is in a developmental phase, receives uncoordinated and irregular funding from multiple sources, is constrained to rely heavily on untrained Caseworkers, has limited access to the social service delivery system, and works with adolescents who have a history of severe problems—such a program is unable to make headway in solving those problems.

We have also learned that, despite these constraints, the program can achieve a pattern of measureable benefits (Indianapolis, 1978–79). However, this success was not repeated when the staff was reduced and a strike cut two months from the school year. (P. 87.)

---

4. Peter Rossi once observed that program evaluation work is held in low esteem by academicians doing basic research (pp. 17–18, 1969).

He went on to discuss an alternative conceptualization or strategy: "solution building." He closed a lengthy review of student cases with the generalizations: "Who is most likely to benefit from CIS? Students who come with at least some sort of asset. The asset can be a strong parent, or the student's existing motivation. . . . The student without any visible assets—with problems at home, no signs of self-starting, behavioral problems, few basic academic skills—may be retrievable, but not by CIS alone" (p. 110).

In the report Murray went no further along this line than: "It is not at all clear that CIS is an answer for any appreciable number of the worst-of-the-worst among the nation's problem youth" (p. 117). But orally (for example, at the Atlanta stakeholder meeting, November 1980) Murray made explicit the *Report's* implication that success was beyond the reach of the CIS approach unless the target group of youngsters was redefined as "less troubled" youngsters. This conclusion was unsettling.

Such a redefinitional conclusion dismayed social scientists on the Technical Review Panel. They believed the data were too few to justify such an important conclusion. It dismayed "liberals," who saw it as punitive, a declaration that the opportunities of education should be shared only among those whom society could recognize as redeemable. It upset school officials in Atlanta and Indianapolis, who saw their own programs as able to help delinquent students who wanted to change, but admitted needing help with students without visible assets. It dismayed CIS people, who saw themselves doing a good job with "worst cases." It threatened the appeal CIS had with funding agencies.

Murray recognized that his data base, including detailed case information on a small number of youngsters, was not sufficient for attribution of effect to the program and not a good basis for grand generalization, positive or negative. Yet the pressures from his colleagues in and outside AIR, his own sense of what a study should accomplish, and his contract made him want to say not only that CIS "did not" but "could not" achieve its aims under these conditions. But in his written reports he only declared that it "did not" and suggested reasons why.

Many readers were interested in what this particular CIS enterprise accomplished and failed to accomplish. For the conclusion that CIS fell short of its stated goals Murray had sufficient data. (It was summarized at the outset of this chapter.)

The major contribution to program development and evaluation to be found in the CIS experience, according to Murray, was the generalization that one should attend to successful provision of program elements or assistances. Following the advocacy of Paul Schwarz, AIR president and senior reviewer for the CIS evaluation study, Murray called this approach "solution building." For compensatory programs, e.g., Cities-in-Schools, where "return" to some norm is sought, heavy emphasis on the norm regularly has resulted in "no-difference" findings and "devaluation" of the program. Murray argued—not from data formally gathered but out of experience and on logical grounds—that any compensatory program should be recognized as partially enabling, possibly even necessary, but certainly not sufficient for elimination of "the problem." Or alone even for its reduction.

Thus Murray drew attention to the success of CIS in providing circumstances (pre-investment accomplishments) that were believed to facilitate "first-turnaround" investments by the students. He emphasized "personalism" and "the caseworker." He did not analyze personalism in a traditional social science or cite literature on diadic counseling relationships and caseworker roles, both heavily researched topics, but provided examples of relationships at CIS sites and interpretations.[5] He concluded that the "family" concept, small caseload structure, and avoidance of a particular problem orientation (an antispecialist view?) facilitated the relationships.

This argument for "solution building" or "incrementalism" follows a tradition in program evaluation sometimes identified with Lee Cronbach (1963) and often labeled "formative evaluation" or "instrumentalism." The emphasis is on leaving those in charge of education and social services in a better position for the next effort. Murray used the analogy: "CIS saw itself as baking pies (having major effects on a student's life). The evaluation was seen as counting how many pies were baked. The more accurate view of the situation is that CIS was the flour. An evaluation that counts pies is never going to be in a position to answer the more pertinent questions: How good is the flour? What else is needed to produce the pie?"

As indicated in the minutes of the retrospective Technical Re-

---

5. Technical Review Panelists Eugene Webb and David Wiley had encouraged Murray to do mini-experiments at single sites to increase the understanding of key factors.

view Panel meeting, this "solution building" rationale was taken by several of the social scientists as "letting CIS off the hook." They insisted on "impact" standards, following a tradition associated with Michael Scriven (1967) and sometimes called "summative evaluation" or "product evaluation." They applauded the fact that Murray had tried to produce knowledge about CIS impact and had in fact demonstrated low impact. Murray felt that to increase the general understanding of CIS he needed to discuss the degree to which CIS had been implemented, but these critics, strong advocates of general-knowledge production, objected because such discussion detracted from the findings of low impact.

### The Extension of Theory

The *Final Report* of the evaluation of Cities-in-Schools has few bibliographic citations and no bibliography. In the large sense it is atheoretical and ahistorical. Other than citations of project documents the primary reference is to AIR President Schwarz's writing on program development and evaluation. Little before and outside the Atlanta, Indianapolis, and New York City projects is described. The conceptual effort was self-contained. The report is a document more of immediate record than of social science research.

Omitted, for example, was the fact that in 1971 Atlanta Superintendent John Letson created a new school, the John F. Kennedy School and Community Center. It was to be a model of social services integration. No mention of that effort appears in the AIR *Final Report*. Community education ("bring the neighborhood into the school!") was a growing specialization across the country during the 1960s and 1970s. It was written about and occasionally studied in a scholarly way.[6] A policy study entitled "the Potential Role of the School as a Site for Integrating Social Services" was prepared for the U.S. Office of Education in 1971 by the Educational Policy Research Center at Syracuse University. It pointed to several benefits of exploration of the idea and reminded that "little is known about the often highly personal and inter-personal ramifications of integrated services. The potential for institutional jealousies and rivalries, prompted by power and authority sensitivities, are almost limitless" (p. 62). The *Final Report* neither invited the reader to attend to that

---

6. Abt Associates, "Comparative Neighborhood Programs: A Synthesis of Research Findings," O.E.O. Contract #B99-4981 (November 1970).

literature nor contributed *directly* to general understanding of "institutional jealousies and rivalries" and other aspects of services integration.

The same can be said regarding AIR attention to the scholarly literature on "urban education," "social rehabilitation of delinquent youth," or "developmental programs under charismatic leadership," all themes important in the CIS experience. The philosopher of social science expects few studies to provide "breakthroughs" in understanding but hopes, rather, that they will make incremental contributions to what is known already. It is not the responsibility of every researcher to summarize what is already known but each should build upon theory and add to the storehouse of factual information, and to the collection of hunches. This study of CIS addressed itself little to that challenge and contributed little to scientific generalization.

Other than the social scientists involved, few evaluation study stakeholders cared about the report's contribution to social science. Of course they wanted the study to be respectable, along the lines that social science research is respectable: sufficiently quantitative, representative, explicitly operationalized, effectively managed. But most wanted the questions to be investigated to be the questions of practitioners, e.g., outreach assignment managers, caseworkers, and project officers in funding agencies. Just as key questions differ from one user group to another, the methods of questioning vary. The original AIR design and personnel assignments were organized to find relationships among quantitative indicators of program operation, but not to fit these relationships into a well-researched, theory-disciplined, knowledge base. And it could not have gone far in that direction. There can be a little social science in a program evaluation study, and a little program evaluation in a social science study, but the purposes are sufficiently different to deny accomplishing much of both in one study. Though atheoretic and ahistorical he was, Charles Murray designed a study which fulfilled his program evaluation contract.

## Utility of the Study

Formal evaluation studies of educational programs are undertaken with the expectation that they will be useful. The investigators, the sponsors, the program staff, and various other stakeholders have different uses to which they may put the studies. The allocation of resources of research varies considerably as different potential uses are considered.

The term "utility" implies usage and the existence of users.[7] Much evaluation designing identifies the primary user as a "decision maker" and implies that the decision maker will be someone having substantial authority, possibly a sponsor—often persons having policy responsibilities for this and other programs. The orientation to decision makers was protested in the Stanford Consortium review of the Struening-Guttentag encyclopedia (in Glass, 1976), partly because it diminished the importance of information useful to stakeholders who had no immediate decisions to make but who wanted to understand the function and worth of the program. Decision making and policy setting are important consequences of evaluation study, but *understanding* alone is a consequence that indicates utility in evaluation studies.

The previous paragraph emphasized the "knowledge" utility of studies. It is important also to take account of the imprimatur of evaluation studies. The fact that evaluation is going on or has been completed can itself be a substantial utility. Program sponsors or directors often make use of the fact that "an evaluation is underway." Regardless of the findings of the study, the fact of having carried out an investigation carries certain sanctions. An evaluated program may be seen as more authentic. Those responsible for authorizing the evaluation may be seen as acting in "a responsible way." The utility of program evaluation includes such imprimaturs.

Evaluation studies also have utility for "signaling" the standards, expectations, and warnings of an authority. Evaluation requirements are messages about emphases and limits. Evaluation designs are indicators as to what will be under scrutiny—in this program and elsewhere. Not only are inputs and outcomes specified, but theories and philosophies are indicated as in or out of favor. One's design of evaluation research indicates much about one's belief in social change and improvement of services. Evaluation research can be said to have utility if its conduct informs people in these ways.

---

7. For more general discussion of metaevaluation utilities see Alkin, Daillak, and White (1979); Braskamp and Brown (1980); and King and Pechman (1982).

Such a broad definition of utility as a criterion for evaluating evaluation studies bothers some people. But Carol Weiss is one research analyst (among others) who has urged a broad construction. Weiss said: "We may like some uses and dislike others, but such judgments should not get in the way. We need to understand the consequences of research and evaluation for organizational practice. Only with a broad-gauge view will we make headway in the endeavor" (1981).

It was useful to federal supporters of Cities-in-Schools to be able to say that the program was being evaluated, that the funding was being handled in an accountable way. It was useful to NIE spokespersons to be able to say that they were contributing to the practical remedy of urban school problems by conducting this evaluation study. It was useful to CIS spokespersons to say, "We are being rigorously evaluated." The AIR evaluation of CIS had these imprimatur and signaling utilities.

Of course, the concept of utility should not be considered only in a positive sense. There can be negative utilities too. Investigation can postpone the delivery of services. Evaluation expenses often draw from operational funds (that was not the case here). The orientation of knowledge in the evaluation study may draw attention away from important realizations and impede needed decisions. The evaluation work may distract and discourage program personnel. As will be discussed in the final section, that disutility did occur here.

The following paragraphs summarize the use made of particular CIS information from the AIR evaluation team.

During the three-year study evaluators provided the program staff and stakeholders with descriptions of program arrangements, activities, and interim accomplishments. Faced with the growing reality of weak and unworkable data on program impact, Charles Murray increasingly portrayed weaknesses of management, staff competence, student selection, and caseworker record keeping. Program directors had been at least partially aware of these deficiencies, but the stimulus to strong remedial action was absent until AIR feedback arrived. Feedback on the ineffectiveness of pursuit of one original goal—to bring about a vital integration of social services—brought no more than the surprising response that this was not an objective of immediate priority.

Data on attendance, achievement, and delinquency—as well as information on the sparsity of such data—were widely distributed within the program. The response was acknowledgment, but improvement seldom followed.

The Indianapolis CIS people responded more directly to the feedback on shortfall than did those at the other two sites. There was feeling in New York and Atlanta, and a mention of it in Indianapolis too, that the evaluators were overly concerned with form, too little concerned with substance. CIS field site people recognized that a CIS organization more uniform from site to site, more fully committed to record keeping, would not necessarily play the *intended* role with youth any better. At the national level of Cities-in-Schools there was a high readiness to respond to the evaluation reports. Even while the AIR study was in progress (and partly because of it), a management information system was established to do similar monitoring within *their own* (CIS's) control.

By the time NIE had printed and circulated the *Final Report* in 1980, the findings were well known.[8] Some people found the conclusions too kind; some thought them too mechanical. I found the conclusions limited in scope, yet coherent, pertinent, interesting, and "contractually" correct. But little use was made of them. Charles Murray was disappointed with the program, with his *Report*, and with the reaction to it. Like CIS itself, the American Institutes for Research had promised more than it delivered. The utility of its evaluation reporting was limited largely to early feedback on operational difficulties.

The *Final Report* was not circulated widely within or outside the program. By the time it was printed and officially released, its findings were over a year old. (Lengthy delays of such reports are not uncommon.) No stakeholder group found it a source of critical planning information or evidence to back a key argument. The *Final Report* was occasionally cited, but its utility as a resource document was negligible.

### The Stakeholders

The nature of the evaluation study was influenced by contemporary notions of research utility. To counter overemphasis on knowledge production, to assure attention to the immediate needs of people

---

8. The interactive nature of Murray's design for stakeholder evaluation had necessitated intermediate and final review of observations and interpretations.

faced with practical responsibility, the stakeholder orientation was set forth in the RFP and repeatedly insisted upon by Norman Gold.

CIS reformers had a large stake in the evaluation study. Not only might AIR's findings increase their understandings, but their political standing and opportunities for support could be enhanced or jeopardized by the study. In this effort to tease out whether or not the evaluation work blunted the reform of social services, it is important to re-examine AIR's commitment to stakeholders.

When Charles Murray spoke to the Evaluation Research Society in Minneapolis in 1977, he emphasized using the stakeholder concept to increase the *use* of evaluation findings: "The fundamental assertion about Stakeholders is that they can increase the likelihood that an evaluation will be used" (p. 2, partial draft of presentation, AIR files). Acknowledging that evaluation studies are often little used, Murray planned to make this CIS evaluation usable and useful.[9] The stakeholder, Murray said:

(1) can tell the evaluator what to measure,
(2) can tell the evaluator when and in what form the evaluation must be presented to be useful, and
(3) will be more likely to pay attention to the evaluation results when they are presented. (P. 2)

This utilitarian orientation did not rule out an evaluator's pursuit of grand generalizations, but gave higher priority to findings pertinent to CIS operations familiar to on-site stakeholders.

In a rationale for stakeholder evaluation prepared at NIE, Norman Gold emphasized concern for the utility of evaluation studies. He alluded to a 1977 report by Stephen Weiner of the Stanford Evaluation Consortium. Entitled "Pathology in Institutional Structures for Evaluation and a Possible Cure," Weiner's paper aimed at "increasing the influence of evaluators." Gold also alluded to contemporary interest in stakeholders as presented in writings by Stake

---

9. Stakeholders are often unrealistic in their presumptions of data utility and usage. To the amusement of the Technical Review Panel, Charles Murray once told of an instance of naive expectation for clear-cut finding and programmatic follow-up. Murray said: "I was stymied at the first White House meeting. I had said, 'We all know that many of the reasons why specific programs survive has nothing to do with technical criteria of success and failure.' The people at the table disagreed, saying, 'No. We will look at the data. If the program is shown to be effective we will make our decision accordingly.' My mouth dropped open. . . ."

on "responsive evaluation," House on concern for "fairness and justice," Stufflebeam on "effective decision-making," and Edwards and Guttentag on representing the "priorities of constituencies" (p. 2, Gold, 1981, draft).

The ERS Technical Review Panel heard Murray's words about increasing the evaluation study's utility. Malcolm Klein and other members seeking generalizable findings did not see the stakeholder approach as requiring a substantial departure from the pursuits of quantitative social science. Stakeholder evaluation was little discussed, and when discussed it was treated unenthusiastically—a constraint, perhaps a challenge, certainly not an opportunity. It was interpreted primarily as a basis for adding to the list of measurable variables. Without diminishing his advocacy of a stakeholder approach, Gold assured the panel at its first meeting that the AIR study was to be a "fundamentally sound piece of research." Everyone believed that everyone would profit by new and penetrating insights on grand multi-city efforts to provide services to urban youth.

Who were the *stakeholders* here? As indicated in Chapter One, Murray (with help from Redish) distinguished between local and national stakeholders. Locals included those deciding resource allocations, the program beneficiaries, and program staff. Nationals included funding agencies, federal policy makers, and evaluation researchers. In practice Murray found it useful to separate the locals into "decision makers" and "consumers," those who were more concerned about the project as a whole against those who directly or indirectly were recipients of program service. Project members such as Mary Jane McConahay and David Lewis were stakeholders not well represented by this arrangement. They had access to Murray's attention if they wanted it, but (unlike in the usual formative evaluation situation) their concerns were not considered high in priority. Officially, CIS staffers were stakeholders, but their conversation with evaluators was to serve the data needs of other stakeholders rather than their own.[10]

The questions AIR used to involve stakeholders were straightforward. Groups regularly were asked:

(1) What indicators would convince you that the project is successful?

---

10. Rodman and Kolodny once identified organizational arrangements which increase the distance between researchers and practitioners (1964). Such arrangements were apparent here.

(2) What are the most important of these indicators for you?
(3) When do you need feedback from the evaluation?
(4) In what form would you prefer that feedback to be? (Janice Redish, p. 4, Preliminary Report on User's Needs, January 1978)

As indicated here and at the outset of Chapter Two, Murray was setting the *evaluation study* as the focal point of the stakeholder approach rather than the stake stakeholders had in the program. He, for example, did not ask them:

(1) What is your stake in CIS?
(2) What do you have to gain or lose?
(3) What about CIS is important to protect?
(4) What about CIS concerns you?

These latter questions would probably have taken the study still further from a test of CIS's general approach, i.e., "personalistic" youth assistance and services integration. Murray's course was a compromise, attendant to the information needs of stakeholders who could identify them, but keeping the needs conceptualized as outcome indicators which would regress on treatment variables.

Community decision makers were comfortable with Murray's information delivery questions. The "consumers" (sometimes called "clients") found the questions hard to answer. Murray said:

The idea of using clients as stakeholders never really got off the ground. How do you get parents and kids together in Indianapolis? You have to use the program to get them together. So what do you get? You get the "Fan Club." You get parents who really like the program. They tell a lot. It's a wonderful data collection device for us because even though they're "fans" you really learn a lot listening to them. But this isn't having a stake in it. I don't see how you establish a stakeholder kind of relationship here. (ERS Panel, Chicago, 1980.)

All through the study Murray was holding meetings with the decision makers. He had more or less abandoned the consumers. They were unhelpful and seemingly uninvolved.[11] He could have served them better. He could have probed their apprehensions. Or he could have conceived issues about which they should have been concerned. He could have given study to questions that aggressively

---

11. In her commissioned evaluation of CIS for the Field Foundation, Judy Austermiller reported that Murray expressed reservations about the effectiveness of the stakeholder panels (unpublished document, 1978; see section on the federal period).

examined the well-being of students, teachers, and citizens, questions like:

(1) With Arsenal Tech's long-standing reputation for vocational education, is it right to deny these CIS students vocational courses, giving them instead an all-day immersion in basic (academic) skill training?

(2) Are ordinary classroom teachers using referral (banishment?) to CIS as a way of diminishing their problems of classroom control?

(3) Are CIS loyalties formed at the expense of family and neighborhood ties?

(4) Are "CIS family" interactions supportive of traditional ethical codes? Are they socially upgrading? Are they at least occasionally intellectually stimulating—as well being personally supportive and skill-developing?

(5) What gaps in social services *still* exist? Are there foolish redundancies?

Beset with many problems, Murray was not looking for ways to expand the study.[12] Working with decision-making stakeholders took time but was rewarding. Working with consumer stakeholders seemed fruitless.

It perhaps is important to note the stakeholder approach here was not carried to the point of probing social costs and fairness of the program. Risk is an essential implication of the word "stakeholder." A stake may be lost. It might be improved. Whether or not the stake is protected, even treated fairly, is part of the concept of stakeholder evaluation—as some see it.[13] The ultimate value of stakeholder approaches to program evaluation will probably involve the fairness and justice of educational and social provisions. These aspects were not studied here.

Stakeholding was perceived here within an information technology model. An advocate might say, "What evaluation studies do is produce information. People should use that information to guide

---

12. Part of the time problem resulted from Murray's interpretation of stakeholder evaluation as stakeholder-participative evaluation. He could have pursued more of their probable concerns and could have spent less time surveying their needs. But that would have diminished the hope of utility (and political safety) through shared ownership.

13. See Ernest House's "Justice in Evaluation."

decision making." According to NIE, what was to be demonstrated by AIR here was the proposition that if stakeholders are drawn into discussions of design and intermediate finding, the ultimate findings will be better used. When we discussed this rationale for his stakeholder approach. Murray and I both invoked several other criteria as well, particularly interim utility and sensitivity to the political role of evaluation research.[14]

In addition to the information generated, evaluation research is undertaken for its imprimatur and signaling uses (as defined in the previous section). Each use introduces additional stakeholders. The federal government in effect announced certain purposes and standards by commissioning this evaluation study. NIE leaders were looking for ways of demonstrating NIE usefulness and integrity. A good evaluation study was expected to help—a bad study could have hurt. Also, the American Institutes for Research could have been a big winner or loser, depending on how the study went. Evaluation Research Society officials took the unusual step (for a professional society of its kind) of contracting to provide an advisory panel. Panel members were not told to represent the organization, yet the organization (and more generally, the professional specialization) was at risk here. So NIE, AIR, and ERS all were stakeholders in the evaluation study. It should be noted again that they were *not* stakeholders in the CIS program but *were* stakeholders in the evaluation project.

The CIS reformers also were stakeholders in the evaluation study. Their interests in some ways coincided with other interests. But in certain ways reformer interests were in direct conflict with interests of the technical groups. NIE, AIR, and ERS had a common interest in producing a respectable piece of research—accurate, objective, tough. Cities-in-Schools people wanted a study that "understood" their true aims, was tolerant of their indifference to proper organization and management practice, commiserated with youngsters facing enormous social displacement, and gave credit for what CIS accomplished without concluding that its people "ought to be more like technocrats and engineers." To further their cause, they wanted not just sympathy, not just acknowledgment, but a "bottom

---

14. That there were also political purposes for this stakeholder approach was apparent in the minutes of the retrospective Technical Review Panel meeting, as reported in the final pages of Chapter Four.

line" so oriented. No respectable evaluator would give them all they wanted, but a stakeholder-based evaluation study should have presented their case more completely.

According to Charles Murray, almost all variables requested by the reformist stakeholders were already listed by the evaluators. Nor did the quality of research questions improve because of the meetings. The stakeholder meetings did apparently contribute to Murray's turn toward more practical matters. He said that the direct contact increased his admiration for their efforts and sympathy for their plight—even, in the eyes of at least one person (see Peter Rossi's comment in Chapter Four), to a certain degree of "co-option." The stakeholder approach appears to have made the evaluators more aware of sources of support and opposition to CIS. Sensitivities apparently were increased.

But in the world of Charles Murray (and most other evaluation researchers) the CIS stakes were small compared to those of AIR, NIE, and ERS. Professional affiliation and accepted standards of inquiry held sway. The *Final Report* acknowledged a certain integrity of the reform effort but declared Cities-in-Schools to be an unsound national investment.

In summary, the evaluation team did not take full advantage of the stakeholder concept, limiting formal consideration largely to "information enhancement." The effort did not improve the selection of issues studied, but did increase team interaction with community people. During the study CIS's use of evaluation feedback was enhanced by decision maker–stakeholder participation, but not after the *Final Report* was prepared. The primary effect of AIR involvement with these stakeholders probably was to draw temporary attention to local use of information and away from the production of generalizable knowledge—but in the end the program was considered not a success because hard evidence of student gain was not obtained.

### Enervating Improvement

The closing sentence of Charles Murray's *Final Report* was: "The more reasonable assumption is that 'an inner-city school that works' will include as part of its resources something very like CIS, and that the most economical way to reach that goal is to build on the start that CIS has made" (p. 120). With these closing lines Mur-

ray intended not only to commend CIS for good intention and se-
lected accomplishments but to diminish the report's negative pall.
A few pages earlier he had indicated that efforts to integrate social
services and bring youth offenders into the mainstream of society
needed more planning and better institutional commitments than
had occurred here. He said that Cities-in-Schools had failed. And
for any such program to succeed, many difficult (but not "exotic")
changes would first have to take place (p. 112).

The possibility that CIS could not have succeeded was raised.
Orally Murray put it bluntly; in writing he was less direct. His was
a devastating hypothesis: all here-and-now CIS-type efforts were
futile. Yet it could be true. In Murray's opinion present federal funding arrangements destined programs to fail.

His readers seemed not to take this notion seriously. CIS might
in fact have been destined to fail, but the local stakeholders, especially when displeased by evaluation findings, continued to believe
that federally funded "youthwork" services could be effective.

People believe that services can improve. Experience tells them
so. Research persuades them little one way or another—experience
and opinion dominate. And it would be their experience with variety
rather than with change and control, rather than with strict covariation, that tells them that services can improve. They do not have to
look far to see that some youth services are more humane, some
more effectively coordinated, some getting more favorable responses
from boys and girls. Even in any one program services get better
and worse over time. "What has been, can be!" Since variety and
change are ever with us, it is easy to believe that providing better
services in any one neighborhood or all across the nation is possible.

Within CIS the ebb and flow of enthusiasm to try was apparent.
And things had to be going right, fair winds blowing, for full enthusiasm to sustain: for a caseworker to keep working not knowing if
paychecks would continue, for a Chamber of Commerce director to
risk hassling with the gangs down there, for a pregnant girl to go
to school. Milliken and his following seemed to thrive on adversity,
but they had their down times. And negative feedback from the
evaluators brought both discouragement and a flurry of activity to
counter the findings.

Especially at first the words from AIR were tentative, couched
in apparent empathy and offers of assistance. But Murray pointed

out organizational disarray and CIS disregard for a host of promises made. What CIS got was not "news." What Murray had to say was already known to be needed but was now increasingly an imposed demand: better management; better student selection; better training of caseworkers; better records of activities, problems, and results.

Even in a novel enterprise such as CIS there are ordinary processes by which some things get done and others ignored. The compulsion within CIS was to get more staff members in closer contact with more youngsters. But no, the evaluators were saying: "hold off, plan ahead, spend more time training, read your own contracts, set up a "program," manage these things. Some CIS people seemed to agree, or at least acquiesced. The evaluators had a modest impact organizationally. Some things were rearranged. A little more time was spent on the records, a little less time was spent on the kids— probably not much changed. Still things were not going as well as they should have been. The evaluators were trying to help—but they were trying mostly to get a research study going. Getting that pregnant girl back in school was not the highest priority for them.

In no way could the AIR contract for evaluation research be construed as technical assistance to Cities-in-Schools. As is usual, however, researchers and clients alike presumed that the information being collected for program evaluation would be useful for program management. And as was stated earlier in the chapter, to an extent it was. Problems in spreading caseworker resources too thin *were* better realized after the first evaluation feedback came in. Murray pressed the feedback on CIS leaders, urging that operational priorities be changed. The program had been adapting to the circumstances at each school, fitting in, changing the original plan, giving the school's principal, for example, a voice in how the services should be arranged. The evaluators complained that the evaluation would not be effective, future expansion would not be soundly based, if "treatment across schools" were not uniform. The credibility of the evaluation was at stake. Future federal funding appeared to be at stake. The advice of the evaluators was not incompatible with CIS's national management *plans*. Ordinary operations *were* changed, at least a little, especially in Indianapolis. Whether or not they were changed for the better remains a debatable question.

Uniformity of treatment remained an important standard with AIR. Rather than accepting CIS as an emergent, locally adaptive process, the evaluators wanted to treat CIS as a generic process, potentially available for placement in all cities. They saw local circumstances already overly dissimilar. Effects were going to be very difficult to measure. The evaluators wanted to diminish the time needed to describe and understand the treatment. Uniformity across schools was not a standard with most program stakeholders—save school administrators and perhaps "the government." Yet uniformity, maintenance of the original written plan, and resistance to local adaptation became indicators of good programming, and were pressed upon CIS fieldworkers.

Good evaluation practice requires some uniformities within the program if representations are to be meaningful, especially if new installations of program concept are anticipated. Good evaluation practice also requires minimal interference in program operation. A balance needs to be found. Here it was clear to me that Murray pushed too hard for uniformity. Several ERS panelists judged Murray's pressure as not hard enough.

Evaluation is a natural, ubiquitous human activity, mostly carried on unconsciously, only occasionally made formal with *specification* of what needs to be known and what was found. From research and experience it is known that in the presence of a greater authority, e.g., a "better developed" evaluation system, individuals will lessen their own surveillance, be less attentive to their own warning signals. It is reasonable to suppose that in the presence of a major evaluative study, some diminution of evaluative surveillance occurred within CIS. (This supposition was neither confirmed nor denied in the interviews.) The power of controlling the repository of feedback data was apparent to CIS board members. Chairman Howard Samuels insisted that CIS institute its own management information system to provide more immediate feedback to the program and, if necessary, to counter hurtful information from federal evaluators. This also might have occurred had there been no federal evaluation study, but to some extent the constraint on informal evaluation and adaptation was apparent. *With* the evaluation, the CIS work was different from what it would have been without it.

The evaluators had a strong idea of what "a program" should be. AIR President Paul Schwarz had indicated that eventually he hoped AIR would have an opportunity to undertake such social action projects itself. They were well acquainted with the social science literature on innovation in education and the social services, the work of Ronald Havelock (1973) and Milbrey McLaughlin (1975), for example. The evaluators recognized the political nature of social work (Morris, 1979) and of evaluation research itself (Cohen, 1970; House, 1974). They were well acquainted with the problems of treating human affairs "rationally" and of expecting too much too soon. Yet the AIR notion was "rational" (and ultimately, I believe, expected too much). It is exemplified by Figure 3, a flow of energy and purpose through planning, operations, production, and feedback. Program activities needed to be stipulated, responsibilities realized, indicators monitored. AIR wanted to be creative about these things, but saw social science constructs as *essential* epistemological structure. If the CIS program was to be a success, if it was to be recommended to American cities, it *would* have such features. To be successful, it had to be describable. It had to be sufficiently uniform so that one description more or less would cover it all.

AIR did not devote a substantial portion of its budget to studying CIS operations so that they would be described most effectively, but Murray and his colleagues overviewed the processes. They did not see a sufficiency of the ingredients they were looking for. They did not see adequate manifestation of a workable central plan. Authority was obscure in CIS. Communication was informal, terms were inadequately defined. Training was haphazard. An ethic of basing future operations on present results was missing.

It is not clear whether traces of the ingredients were too subtle, too idiosyncratic—or whether the ingredients were missing. Murray soon presumed that it was clear that CIS was not going to be exportable to other cities, so he worried little about looking longer. There really is no dispute about one conclusion: management was one of CIS's weakest features.

In response to first-year charges of weak management, Elizabeth Baltz was asked to reorganize management of the Indianapolis project. Later she moved on to help run the national office. For reasons unclear, she was considered by some an interloper. She talked Murray's language; to some that alone seemed to make her a threat to "the real CIS." The more I heard the complaints the more I came to believe that what the corporate world sees as "good management" is not highly compatible with the central CIS ethic and offering: personalistic youthwork.

Howard Samuels had dedicated himself to running Cities-in-Schools as a business should be run. Burton Chamberlain was brought in as executive vice-president to set up a more competent program management. As far as I could see, neither of them (nor Charles Murray) dealt with the incompatibility in the two purviews. For the neighborhoods where CIS will be, good caseworkers are seldom going to be good record keepers. Ghetto fieldwork and corporate management have essential frictions. What is best for CIS is not always the corporate view.

Murray did not choose to study just how removed CIS management was from optimal management of the unique work being done. Early CIS management (and some later on) was considered disordered and negligent, particularly for failing to insist that the ideal CIS would be a unified, centrist program.

In a similar AIR evaluative study of federal support for Jesse Jackson's PUSH-to-Excellence project, Saundra Murray concluded that Jackson had never established "a program" (1982). Uniform activities, objectives, and accounting of results were not to be found in the several cities monitored. In a case study of the evaluation work (a companion piece to this one) Farrar and House (1982) stated that Jackson had never claimed to have a "program," that federal officials had defined it such so that they could fund his work under existing legislation, that it was more a movement than a program, and that it was held up to criteria that emerged from social science notions of "program" ill suited to a spiritualistic and inspirational movement. It is seldom that evaluators are challenged as to whether or not they used the right criteria, but it occurred with PUSH/Excel.

It happened again and again with Cities-in-Schools, but seldom in public. In the pain of first knowledge of AIR findings William Milliken moaned, "But did they ask the right questions?" Charles Murray reminded us that Milliken had countless opportunities to identify the right questions. Murray believed there were no better questions. Milliken knew that the worth of what he was doing was not indicated in Murray's data. Some people who know them both say that it must be possible for both to be right.

### The Quieting That Occurred

Let me summarize the case I have tried to make in this book. It seems clear to me that CIS program people changed some practices, responding to suggestions (demands?) made by the evaluators. Certainly some discouragement followed evaluation feedback throughout the period. The evaluators believed that there was good reason to be discouraged and claimed that only with better organization could reform occur and could the reform be evaluated. To various degrees CIS program people both agreed and disagreed with the evaluator's claim.

It seems clear to me that the program people—these urban reformers—did turn away somewhat from previous experience, from their intuitive plan for providing support to the youth. Those who agreed to the evaluator-recommended changes felt that they might thus facilitate long-term expansion of CIS services. At least for the present, that expansion did not occur and the teams drifted apart. The concept of noneducator caseworkers working full-time in the schools, of all the city's social forces in "personalistic" collaboration, has largely disappeared. The reform quieted. It did not end, but it quieted.

Activities had at times been frenzied. Some quieting was welcome. Most CIS people agreed that better training and better record keeping were needed. It would take a while to get these in place. This was a quieting for the organization's good—but there was another. Some caseworkers and managers were disheartened. It was a while before some could throw themselves into it again; some dropped out.

Still another CIS reaction to the evaluation was contention. "How can we dismiss Murray's claims? How can we nullify this bad press?" Milliken attacked the criteria as simplistic. Joyce McWilliams wrote the rebuttal and prepared a "survival kit" for CIS spokespersons. Howard Samuels and Burton Chamberlain instituted CIS's own management information system. However needed or valid these responses, they were largely a response to the power of social science research to shape CIS destiny. Cities-in-Schools people diverted energies from something they were experts at (getting funds and developing personal relationships with the ghetto's problem youth) to address their organizational frailties. The reform work was quieted as CIS mobilized to defend itself. Some of the quieting was an indication of program debilitation.

*What is not clear is how much the evaluative research operation contributed to the debilitating quiet.* The evidence is good that the evaluation study had an effect, but I cannot separate the debilitating quiet from the restorative quiet.

CIS leaders were attentive to AIR feedback. Some staff members were defensive, some organized something of a counterattack.

They denied the accuracy of certain findings. Some were inclined to boycott the evaluation activity. The evaluation was a distraction, a continuing distraction. Some interesting charges were raised: that AIR fixed its gaze upon too few criteria, had set standards too high, had been overly fearful of recidivism, etc. The communal interest of evaluation research and innovative programming was called into question. The program was obligated to draw away from what it saw to be its work to attend to what it was not very good at doing.

There are alternative reasons why CIS activities peaked and began to wane. Funding was at risk because the government had other attentions. Opponents in each city opposed CIS continuation. Charles Murray was a convenient scapegoat. The evidence that the AIR evaluation caused the downfall of CIS activity is almost non-existent. It is not clear that AIR contributed to the debilitating quiet of reform but also not clear that it did not.

One argument, voiced by Charles Murray, is that the program was not effective the way it was, that it was not even ready to be evaluated, that it *should* have been quieted, or at least allowed time without evaluation to straighten itself out. He thought that the evaluation data contributed to a needed realization—and, yes, to a quieting.

An alternative argument, more or less William Milliken's, was that CIS was in fact operating effectively on a person-by-person basis, that it was the recording-keeping-for-evaluation that was not working, that the demands of the evaluators drew substantial energies from the personalized support system, and that if a true assessment were possible, it would show that CIS was doing as well as our society knows how, to move these youth toward productivity and respect in their communities.

As long as the evaluators and others maintained the view that AIR was providing at least an approximation of a true assessment, their lack of impact data and lack of support for CIS fieldwork probably contributed to diminution of the reform efforts. The evidence for this diminution is not strong. I looked for it and found nothing we would call causal evidence. Obviously at times efforts waned, and in the end the program in two cities greatly diminished, yet in the third, New York City, it took new life. I cannot conclude that the evaluative research effort quieted the reform, but I leave it to the reader as a possibility.

Another question remains as to whether AIR worked with standards set too high. It is not clear that every minimally successful CIS project *would* produce gains in reading scores and cutback in absenteeism and trouble with the law.[15] Suppose that some small change in "life perspective" did occur in each of the youngsters in CIS: a movement toward accepting common social values.[16] Somehow the changes might, but would not necessarily, show up on Murray's indicators.

What is minimal expectation for a $2,000 additional investment in an urban youth already in trouble? Or to put the issue more generally—as Jarvis Barnes did in Chapter Four—what is the cost effectiveness of Cities-in-Schools? For certain dollar costs, what minimum returns should we expect? How much should we as a society be willing to pay for small movements toward social acceptability?

We who are social scientists should be able to help people answer these questions. Perhaps we should be able to say what can be accomplished for what costs. But we cannot. Some specialists pretend to, but their estimates are presumptuous. With regard to innovative social and educational programs we cannot provide basic cost-effectiveness information.

The Cities-in-Schools situation at first appeared to provide one of the best opportunities ever to put a price tag on a few social service and educational arrangements. But not even the "pure form" was reduced to economic equation. Nor would it have been had Murray collected every datum identified in his full-blown proposal. And it is not reasonable to suggest that other researchers could have done the job proposed. It was not a failing of design or staffing.

It is reasonable to believe that for such services there is no way of determining cost figures that will generalize to different cities, across different administrations, remaining invariant as federal and local backup programs vary over time. It *is* important for us to conceptualize the problem as one of costs and benefits, but it is not reasonable for us to expect that for such programs, sound, useful cost-benefit data can be provided.

For district and federal decision making we will have to continue following the usual iterative process, asking—with careful

15. The AIR program evaluation rationale cautioned against setting too high a standard and advocated a more gradualistic turnabout.

16. Such changes would not necessarily be attributable to CIS, of course. Adolescents do mature. Some changes for the better would occur without social service intervention.

consideration of the distress—how much we can afford to spend, then asking how best can we use our funds to adjust our present services, back and forth.[17] It is irresponsible to say we should decide on the program needed, then find the money to pay for it. Responsible decisions are made by intuitive compromise among need, resources, and a program's potential for solution of the problems. To effect these compromises we need program indicators such as Murray gathered. And we also need to know more about day-to-day operations and more about individual caseworker-student interactions.

William Milliken told of the youngster who did not begin talking to his youthworker until after months of silence. Joyce Mc-Williams told of the 14-year-old girl with multiple physical problems, chronically absent, without parental backup—who came to CIS on her own, was tutored, shepherded, represented—who now had won a class math prize. There is no dispute as to whether or not these things happened. Charles Murray recognized such cases, but could not find evidence that collectively the youth were making substantial and enduring improvement. He looked for the evidence and found little. Still he concentrated on written records, not getting personally involved in individual cases.[18] Murray granted that commendable youth support occurred, but added that it did not aggregate to produce durable improvement in the youngsters, especially as evidenced in the three agreed-upon criteria.

At the outset, with concurrence from others, Murray had set what he considered to be standards easy to attain. CIS did not attain them. Neither Murray nor other evaluators continued to raise the issue as to whether or not those standards actually had been suitable. They *were* seen as suitable by many people in and out of Cities-in-Schools. Howard Samuels continued to endorse them—but he, too, could have been setting standards too high. The Milliken team asked, "Do such expectations adequately consider the uniqueness of a child's deviant behavior and the uniqueness of a restorative path? Or mostly reveal our wishes as to what the world should be?"

---

17. The notion of zero-base budgeting for social services comes not from practical experience but from desire that costs and services be drastically cut knowing that poorly defined services are vulnerable, even when valued.

18. In *Street Corner Society* W. F. Whyte indicated that a researcher had to be "hanging around" to discover what was happening in young people's lives.

Many CIS people said in effect that AIR standards were too high—the "walls too thick," the problems too complex, the road back too tortuous. They said the evaluators' thinking was just not compatible with their work. They had acquiesced earlier on the matter of standards because they, too, thought CIS would accomplish them and because they had no sense of the technical difficulty in using *common* criteria with students having greatly uncommon problems.

Is it possible that these fieldworkers were more right than the technical experts? Could their accomplishments, however poorly recorded, have been a source of national pride, even with disappointment that more was not accomplished? Should not the obligation to work with the youngsters continue, using the best people and ideas, with what resources we can afford, even if we are unable to measure the impact? Surely the evaluators should not decide the question of continuance, but they and the public should examine the logic connecting a shortfall on specified criteria with decisions to discontinue the effort.

The CIS fieldworkers seemed genuine in their belief that sometimes they made a difference—to be sure, in different ways with different kids. Some of them admitted that their organization had many deficiencies. But with many caseworkers and youngsters, they believed the additional "investment" paid off. One of the reasons the Carters are no longer in the White House is that they also believed these $2,000 purchases were reasonable. It seems indirectly that the majority of voters thought otherwise. Here in Reagan's first term, if United Way, the churches, and the schools cannot deal with the problems of urban youth, the country seems to have little confidence that federally funded social services can. The reform has quieted.

On one point the public, the scientists, and the federal establishment seem to agree. It will not be sufficient for Cities-in-Schools to draw deviant youth slightly toward socially approved behavior. To be deemed successful and to be continued, CIS needs to change children in ways that can be registered for skeptics to see. For things we personally are involved with, it is sufficient to have "experiential knowing" of their success. But for things we are distant from, geographically or culturally, we will require more than testimony. We will require (not just prefer, but require) formal evidence.

And that may mean we will go without sustained social reform efforts.

Knowing and Believing

It seems clear to me that the CIS program people and the AIR evaluation people did not agree on how reform works. They certainly did not agree about ways of recognizing whether or not reform is working. Formal criteria—relatively constant across people and places, not adapted to situations—are a central notion in most formal evaluation designs. CIS program people were inclined to carry out their work as obstacles permitted, then to decide whether or not they were making headway.

The program people agreed to demonstrate their effectiveness nationally, in fact asked for the opportunity to do so. But many of them did not understand that "effectiveness" is an econometric term. They did not comprehend what constitutes "a demonstration."

The on-site Cities-in-Schools staff perception of "effectiveness" was of services rendered, clients engaged, hurts mended. The science-government definition of "program effectiveness" was more in terms of information generated, information to be taken as evidence that funds were properly spent, results recorded, with a basis set for directing subsequent programs.

This latter way is a formal knowing, one that can be shared with a distant stranger—who indeed may work within a very different context. The earlier way was a personal knowing, Polanyi's tacit knowing (1962), an experience and private confidence. The knowing may be revealed in storytelling. But when there are many, many stories, the overall message is unlikely to be clear.

The project people did not understand the demonstration process the way the dissemination experts defined it. The CIS group wanted the benefits of demonstration funding and its opportunity for growth. They accepted the language and its implicit overpromising. They found the terms of program specification, institution building, and evaluative criteria somewhat amusing but not without meaning. But they did not realize how compelling would be the science-technology metaphors of effectiveness, productivity, and impact—pre-empting their own practitioner metaphors and valuings.

As have many philosophers of science, Abraham Kaplan distinguished between social science knowledge and common knowledge: "Scientific observation is deliberate search, carried out with care and forethought, as contrasted with the casual and largely passive perceptions of every day life. It is this deliberateness and control of the process of observation that is distinctive of science, not merely the use of special instruments (important as they are)" (p. 126, 1964).

Studying generalizations to be drawn from evaluation studies, Trumbull and I (1982) have noted the difference between social science knowledge and common knowledge as to their attachment to context. The social scientist searches for the parsimonious, the most context-free generalization, and treats as greatest in authority the information that has been gathered over a variety of contexts, indifferent to them all. The users of common knowledge (including scientists, of course) recognize the interaction of fact with context, the conditional nature of most important generalizations, and treat as most authoritative that knowledge which emanates from a context most relevant to the discussion at hand. The boundary line between general and social science knowledge is indistinct, but most evaluation specialists claim that the latter—more deliberately produced and less contextually bound—is preferable. Few clients are allowed to doubt that what is being offered by the social scientist is higher quality information. Science is said to provide a greater expression of authority.

Charles Lindblom and David Cohen have argued persuasively that social science knowledge cannot be authoritative without verification through common knowledge and that the pursuit of independently authoritative scientific knowledge is a misperception of the social scientists' responsibility (1979). Practitioners know that there are many more issues to consider than those the evaluator entertains, but the evaluator is indignant if his/her issues are not considered the prevailing ones. Especially when the practitioner is expected to identify central issues, he or she is reluctant to argue that the evaluators's plan is off target. In a world where everything is seen to be related to everything else, the evaluator makes a persuasive case that these few indicators can be counted on to represent a great variety of concerns. The practitioner is often quieted—and usually takes steps to assure that his/her performance *on those indicators* will be as robust as possible.

So, during program operation there is a considerable reactive effect—the evaluation work drawing operational pursuits toward a new "bottom line," i.e., what will be measured on the evaluator's instruments. Sometimes that will enhance the program's services. Not always. In the provision of social service there are always bottoms below bottom lines. Ultimate good is sometimes put off by the pursuit of immediate goals.

The key question here is what was the lasting effect of the evaluation presence. The question could be extended further: Did CIS emerge as a better force in its cities because of the evaluation? Were CIS reformers strengthened in their resolve and practice? Or still more grandly, have the many evaluation studies of Great Society programs improved the country's effort to reduce poverty and crime and enhance education and well being?

Formal evaluation probably did not make CIS a better program. In retrospect AIR appears to have contributed to a malaise, a distraction. Cause and effect are not clear. It is apparent that little direct attention was paid to the several AIR evaluation reports. (So it has been with most evaluation studies countrywide.) It is also apparent that the vitality of the effort to reform diminished, locally and beyond. There are surely many causes. It is reasonable to suppose that an unrealistic presumptuousness about what could be expected from federal remedial efforts contributed to present disillusionment. It is reasonable to conclude that the social scientist's literal operationalizations of goal aspirations and reliance on common gain as the indicator of success possibly has contributed as well.

Whether or not CIS deserved to survive is not a key factor in perceiving how social science may be part of the problem in social reform. This case study contributes little to perceptions of the essential worth and usefulness of Cities-in-Schools. Nor does it do much, of course, to resolve the worth and usefulness of social science. What it should have done is help clarify questions about evaluating social programs. The study helped us identify problems that accompany a strong orientation to "information" as a basis for decision making, problems that accompany research aimed at the production of generalizations, and problems that accompany rationality in a reform environment. Whether or not social science and its strongholds, such as AIR, ERS, and NIE, need themselves to reform does not depend on whether or not CIS deserves to survive.

Social science has been essential both to program development and evaluation. The danger that occurs to the observer of the evaluation of Cities-in-Schools is not reliance, but overreliance, on social science. Its thinking—disciplined and dispassionate at its best— provides much less than a complete guide to practice. When working with practitioners program evaluators have often been too much the advocates of social science knowledge, too little the facilitators of joint respect for scientific and experiential knowing. Evaluators should bring their best skeptical scrutinies to bear on their own role in social reform, on their attacks against "personalistic" reformers, and on their support for technocracy.

Administrators know that one way to blunt criticism is to appoint a study committee. Some years ago civil rights agitators came to realize that philanthropic foundations supporting their cause through "studies" succeeded in putting off action rather than fostering it. One intent of rational discourse is to quiet the shouting. Evaluation findings can provoke action, but much more often they postpone (and sometimes, in fact, terminate) action. Are we a better people shouting to right the wrongs or proceeding quietly with resolve? Evaluation philosophy presumes the latter.

But resolve is all too delicate, all too much a creation of its environment. Who pursues good intention without recollection, even without painful recollection? Today's painful recollection is that "it can't be done." We live in an age of constant communication. We know the excessive rainfall of the 48 contiguous states. We know the disorders of North Miami and the West Bank. Almost immediately we know of the world's calamities.

Silently it is announced that all the world's troubles are our troubles, that they are inevitable and unstoppable, that we are *spectators*. The impetus for reform diminishes.

In a minor way formal evaluation research contributes to the disillusionment. And so it strives. It seeks to help us shed our illusions. But without illusion we would find little worthy of attention. A world without curiosity and the aspiration to change, without the hope of "doing good," would rival any prospective calamity. Like the little blue engine, a nation needs to puff, "I think I can."

Program evaluation, as we social scientists have devised it, as Charles Murray and many others of us have practiced it, does little to keep those hopes alive. And sometimes, as here with Cities-in-Schools, it helps to muffle them.

# Bibliography

## AIR Reports

Krug, Robert, Charles Murray, and Jane Schubert. *Evaluation Designs for Cities-in-Schools. Technical Proposal.* Washington, D.C.: American Institutes for Research, 8 September 1977.

Murray, Charles, et al. *The National Evaluation of the Cities-in-Schools Program: Evaluation Design.* Washington, D.C.: American Institutes for Research, May 1978.

Murray, Charles, et al. *The National Evaluation of the Cities-in-Schools Program. Report No. 2: The Program and the Process.* Washington, D.C.: American Institutes for Research, May 1979.

Murray, Charles, et al. *The National Evaluation of the Cities-in-Schools Program. Report No. 3: Program Impact, 1978–79.* Washington, D.C.: American Institutes for Research, October 1980.

Murray, Charles, Blair Bourque, and Susan Mileff. *The National Evaluation of the Cities-in-Schools Program. Report No. 4: Final Report.* Washington, D.C.: American Institutes for Research, 1981.

Redish, Janice, and Jane Schubert. *The National Evaluation of the Cities-in-Schools Program. Report No. 1: Program Descriptions.* Washington, D.C.: American Institutes for Research, February 1978.

## Other References

Alkin, Marvin, Richard Daillak, and Peter White.. 1979. *Using Evaluations: Does Evaluation Make a Difference.* vol. 76, Sage Library of Social Research. Beverly Hills: Sage Publications.

Braskamp, Larry, and Robert Brown, eds. 1980. *New Directions for Program Evaluation.* No. 5, "Utilization of Evaluative Information." San Francisco: Jossey-Bass Publishers.

Brophy, Michael, Stephen Maisto, Leigh Burstein, and Adrian Chan. 1979. "Evaluation of Community Action Programs: Issues and an Alternative." In Robert Coursey et al., eds., *Program Evaluation for Mental*

165

*Health: Methods, Strategies and Participants.* New York: Gruen and Stratton.

Cameron, Kim, "The Enigma of Organizational Effectiveness." 1981. In D. Baugher, ed., *New Directions for Program Evaluation: Measuring Effectiveness.* No. 11. San Francisco: Jossey-Bass Publishers.

Cities-in-Schools. 1977. "An Integrated System of Human Services Delivery" (a.k.a. the "Blue Book.") Washington, D.C.

Cohen, David, 1970. "Politics and Research: Evaluation of Social Action Programs in Education." *Review of Educational Research* 40, no. 2: 213–38.

———. 1983. "Evaluation and Reform." In Anthony Bryk, ed., *New Directions for Program Evaluation.* No. 17, "Stakeholder-Based Evaluation." San Francisco: Jossey-Bass Publishers.

Cronbach, Lee. 1963. "Course Improvement through Evaluation." *Teachers College Record* 64, no. 3: 672–83.

———. 1982. *Designing Evaluations of Educational and Social Programs.* San Francisco: Jossey-Bass Publishers.

Educational Policy Research Center at Syracuse University. 1971. *The Potential Role of the School as a Site for Integrating Social Services.* Syracuse, N.Y.

Edwards, Ward, Marcia Guttentag, and Kurt Snapper. 1975. "A Decision-Theoretic Approach to Evaluation Research." In Elmer Struening and Marcia Guttentag, eds., *Handbook of Evaluation Research*, vol. 1. Beverly Hills: Sage Publications.

Farrar, Eleanor, and Ernest House. 1983. "The Evaluation of PUSH/Excel: A Case Study." In *New Directions for Program Evaluation.* No. 17. San Francisco: Jossey-Bass Publishers.

Glass, Gene, ed. 1976. *Evaluation Studies Review Annual*, vol. 1 Beverly Hills: Sage Publications.

Gottfredson, Michael. 1979. "Treatment Destruction Techniques." *Journal of Research in Crime and Delinquency*, pp. 39–54.

Guba, Egon. 1978. *Toward a Methodology of Naturalistic Inquiry in Educational Evaluation.* Los Angeles: Center for the Study of Evaluation, UCLA Graduate School of Education, University of California.

Hamilton, David. 1977. Making Sense of Curriculum Evaluation: Continuities and Discontinuities in an Educational Idea. *Review of Research in Education* 5: 318–47.

Havelock, Ronald. 1973. *The Change Agent's Guide to Innovation in Education.* Englewood Cliffs, N.J.: Educational Technology Publications.

House, Ernest. 1974. *The Politics of Educational Innovation.* Berkeley: McCutchan Publishing.

———. 1976. "Justice in Evaluation." In Gene Glass, ed., *Evaluation Studies Review Annual*, vol. 1. Beverly Hills: Sage Publications.

———. 1977. "The Logic of Evaluative Argument." Los Angeles: Center for the Study of Evaluation, UCLA.

Joint Committee on Standards for Educational Evaluation. 1981. *Standards for Evaluations of Educational Programs, Projects, and Materials.* New York: McGraw Hill.

Kaplan, Abraham. 1964. *The Conduct of Inquiry.* San Francisco: Chandler Publishing.

Kennedy, Mary. 1982. *Working Knowledge.* Cambridge: Mass.: Huron Institute.

King, J. A., and Ellen Pechman. 1982. *The Process of Evaluation Use in Local School Settings.* Final Report NIE 81-0900. New Orleans Public Schools.

Kurtz, Howie. 1978. "How Chip Carter Got His New Job." *Washington Monthly* (June): 10–17.

Lindblom, Charles, and David Cohen. 1979. *Usable Knowledge: Social Science and Social Problem Solving.* New Haven: Yale University Press.

McLaughlin, Milbrey. 1975. *Evaluation and Reform.* Cambridge: Ballinger Publishing.

Morris, Robert. 1979. *Social Policy of the American Welfare State.* New York: Harper & Row.

Murray, Charles. 1979. Paper presented at the Evaluation Research Society Symposium on Interactive Evaluation, Minneapolis, Minnesota.

Murray, Saundra, et al. 1982. *Final Report* (PUSH-for-Excellence Program) Washington, D.C.: American Institutes for Research, March.

Osborne, John. 1978. "White House Watch: Family Affairs." *New Republic* (October 14): 10–12.

Parlett, Malcolm, and David Hamilton. 1976. *Program Evaluation as Illumination: A New Approach to the Study of Innovatory Programs.* Centre for Research in the Educational Sciences Occasional Paper No. 9. Edinburgh: Centre for Research in the Educational Sciences, University of Edinburgh, 117, 23.

Perloff, Robert, ed. 1979. *Evaluation Interventions, Pros and Cons*, vol. 2. Sage Research Progress Series in Education. Beverly Hills: Sage Publications.

Polanyi, Michael. 1962. *Personal Knowledge: Towards a Post-Critical Philosophy.* Chicago: University of Chicago Press.

Redish, Janice. 1978. *Preliminary Report on Users Needs.* Photocopy draft, January.

Rodman, H., and R. L. Kolodny. 1964. "Organizational Strains in the Research-Practitioner Relationship." *Human Organization* 23: 177–82.

Rossi, Peter. 1979. "Evaluating Educational Programs." *Urban Review* 3, no. 4: 17–18. New York: Center for Urban Education.

Schmuck, Donald. 1967. "Social Psychological Factors in Knowledge Utilization." In *Knowledge Production and Utilization in Educational Administration*, pp. 150–73. CASEA, University of Oregon.

Schön, Donald. 1982. *The Reflective Practitioner.* New York: Basic Books.

Schubert, William. 1980. "Recalibrating Educational Research: Toward a Focus on Practice." *Educational Research* 1, no. 1.

Schwarz, Paul. 1980. "Program Evaluation: Can the Experiment Reform?"

In *New Directions for Program Evaluation.* No. 6. San Francisco: Jossey-Bass Publishers.

Scriven, Michael. 1967. "The Methodology of Evaluation." In Robert E. Stake, ed., *Perspectives of Curriculum Evaluation,* pp. 39–83. AERA Monograph Series on Curriculum Evaluation, No. 1. Chicago: Rand McNally.

———. 1974. *Evaluation: A Study Guide for Educational Administrators.* Nova University, Fort Lauderdale, Fla.

Smith, Louis. 1978. "An Evolving Logic of Participant Observation, Educational Ethnography and Other Case Studies." In Lee Shulman, ed., *Review of Research in Education,* vol. 6. Chicago: Peacock Press.

Smith, Louis, and David Dwyer. 1979. *Federal Policy in Action: A Case Study of an Urban Education Project.* National Institute of Education, U.S. Department of Education, October.

Stake, Robert. 1978. "The Case Study Method in Social Inquiry." *Educational Researcher* 7, no. 2.

———. 1981. "A Needed Subjectivity in Educational Research." *Discourse* 1, no. 2.

Stake, Robert, and Deborah Trumbull. 1982. "Naturalistic Generalizations." *Review Journal of Philosophy and Social Science* 7.

Stenhouse, Lawrence. 1981. "Using Case Study in Library Research." *Social Science Information Studies* 1: 1–10.

Stufflebeam, Daniel, et al. 1971. *Educational Evaluation and Decision Making.* Itasca, Ill: Peacock Publishing.

Von Wright, Georg. 1971. *Explanation and Understanding.* London: Routledge and Kegan Paul.

Weiss, Carol. 1981. "Measuring the Use of Evaluation." In J. Ciaro, ed., *Utilizing Evaluations.* Beverly Hills: Sage Publications.

Wholey, J. S. 1979. *Evaluation, Promise, and Performance.* Washington, D.C.: Urban Institute.

Whyte, William. 1955. *Street Corner Society.* Chicago: University of Chicago Press.

# Index

Absenteeism, 12, 48, 65, 79
Abt Associates, 139
Academic goals, 80, 94
Academic progress, 123
Access, 48
Accountability, 100, 107
Accuracy of reports, 15
Achievement, student, 35, 48, 63,
    86, 107, 119, 149
Admissions, 12, 47, 61, 65, 72, 79,
    109, 137, 151
Adversity, 150
Advocacy, 17, 34, 62, 110, 111
Agencies, 129
    coordination, 115
    integration. *See* Services
        integration
    participation, 93
Aggregation, 134
AIR, 255ff. and *passim*
    findings, 136ff.
    personnel load, 52, 55
    staff turnover, 107
    task analysis, 51
Alcohol use, 46
Allocation of resources, 141
American Institutes for Research.
    *See* AIR
Analyses, statistical, 53, 79, 81, 110
Annala, Ellen, 115
Anonymity, xi
Arrests, 58, 63–66

Arsenal Tech. H.S., 12, 48, 50, 58,
    62, 71, 107, 114
Atlanta schools, *passim*
Attendance, 63, 78, 79, 86, 96
Attitudes, 105, 107, 116
Attribution of cause, x, 26–27, 31,
    34, 35, 42, 50, 56, 58, 73, 79,
    81, 155, 156
Attrition, 95
Audiences, 30, 80, 141
Audit function, 44, 100
Austermiller, Judy, 18, 146
Authority, 161

Baltz, Elizabeth, 32, 48, 53, 86, 101,
    103, 108, 153
Barnes, Jarvis, xii, 64, 113, 157
Bennett, Gerald, 18
Bethlehem, Pa., schools, 97
Bias, xi, 34, 87, 100, 101, 134
Blue Book, 18, 36
Borque, Blair, 52, 55, 105
Boycott, 94, 103, 108, 156
Branch, Helen, 32, 53, 64, 115
Brock, Timothy, 33, 76–78
Bryk, Anthony, 5
Budget, 55
Bureaucratic context, 15, 17ff., 109,
    112, 116

Calendar, xiv, 8, 33, 43, 46, 51
Califano, Joseph, 4, 18, 70

169

Carter, Chip, 21, 87
Carter, Jimmy, 4, 15–18, 70, 81, 87,
    91, 144, 159
Carter, Rosalynn, 16, 18, 23, 48, 87
Carver H.S., 117
Case
    data, 50, 70, 89, 101, 130, 158
    record keeping, 38, 49, 143, 151
    study methods, x, 121, 130
    team, 5, 41, 48, 58, 60, 78
Caseworkers, 11, 50, 83, 91, 94, 138
    training, 60, 61, 136, 151
Causality. *See* Attribution of cause
CETA, 60, 88, 94, 107
Chamberlain, Burton, 13, 29, 86,
    94, 102, 153, 155
Charisma, 9, 112, 120, 122, 140, 154.
    *See also* Messianic leadership
Christian orientation, 16, 35
Cities-in-Schools .
    activities, xiv, 89, 117, 129
    Board, 13, 14, 100, 109
    concept, 45, 47, 57, 61, 77ff., 100,
        109, 122, 125, 129, 133, 146, 152
    contributors, 14, 23
    deficiencies, 142
    families, 5, 48, 58, 78, 89, 138
    management, 49, 61, 94, 129, 151
    National Office, 97, 102
    national staff, 86, 101, 129, 151,
        153
    organization, 112, 113
    potential, 136
    promises, 130, 150
    rationale. *See* CIS concept
    staff, 15, 102, 103, 145
Clark, Kenneth, 33
Cleveland, Barbara, 117
Cohen, David, 5, 76, 161
Communication, 115, 153, 163
Community, 146, 149
    activities, 50
    education, 139
    support, 38
Comparison groups, 57, 74, 102,
    121–23
Competency scores. *See*
    Achievement
Compromises, 158
Conditionality, 161
Confirmation. *See* Validation

Confrontation, 89, 101, 110, 112
Consumerism, 132
Consumers, 145, 146
Contextuality, xii, 41, 46, 74, 91, 99,
    106, 132, 134, 139, 157, 161
Contracts with districts, 41, 64, 116,
    131
Contributors, 14, 23
Cooley, William, 33, 76, 78, 84,
    124–27
Cooption, 74, 81, 102, 122–25, 131,
    149
Cost-benefit, 91, 113, 118, 130, 157,
    160
Costs, 23, 35, 39, 54, 59, 86, 91, 95,
    102, 126
Cotton, Richard, 18
Counseling, 138
Credibility, 112
Crim, Alonzo, 17
Criteria, 112, 131, 149, 159, 160. *See
    also* Design
Criterion referencing, 123
Cronbach, Lee, x, 33, 138, 141
Cycle of failure, 36

Data
    analysis, 53, 79, 81, 110
    base. *See* Data files
    feedback. *See* Information
        feedback
    files, 27, 40, 48, 49, 53ff., 64, 79–
        83, 86, 91, 96, 105, 110, 116,
        121–42
    plan. *See* Design
Davis, Sarah, 107
Dawson, Judy, xi
Decision makers, 83, 132, 141, 149
Decision making, 145, 158
Delayed effects, 102, 105, 113
Delinquency, 35, 65, 66, 95, 140
Demonstration, 5, 9, 17, 35, 56, 59,
    61, 70, 81, 119, 126, 135, 160
Denny, Terry, xi
Descriptive date, 126, 132
Design evaluation, 8, 27, 34ff., 49,
    56, 67, 73, 80, 106, 107, 110,
    125, 132ff.
Destined to fail, 150
Development outcomes, 36, 123
Disappointment, 143

Discouragement, 150, 154, 163
Dissemination, 30, 69, 80, 85, 90,
    93, 119, 162
District contracts, 41, 64, 105
Douglass, William, 110
Drug use, 46

Edmonds, Ronald, 13
Edwards, Ward, 33, 72–82, 121, 145
Election, presidential, 88, 89
Eligibility. *See* Admissions
Emphatic understanding, xi
Empathy for reform, 85, 114, 150, 162
Enrichment activity, 93
Enrollments, 12, 50, 61, 95
Equity, 132
Error types, 131
ERS
    annual meeting, 88, 101, 115, 116,
        119, 125, 144
    credentials, 77
    panel. *See* Technical Panel
Esprit de corps, 78
Evaluability, 44, 127, 156
Evaluation
    design. *See* Design evaluation
    faults, 104
    issues. *See* Research questions
    Network, 69
    proposal, 25ff.
    purposes, 32
    reports, 8
    Research Society, 4, 32, 69, 71,
        125. *See also* ERS
    staffing, 104, 116
    standards, 44
    tools, 103
Evaluator
    constraint, 82
    pressure, 61
Evolution
    of CIS, 151
    program, 131, 132
Exodus, 17, 103, 104, 107
Experiential knowing, 159, 162
    verification, 161
Experiment, 9, 17, 18, 26, 35, 56,
    57, 72, 74, 118, 126
Explanation. *See* Attribution of
    cause
Explication, 153

Failing, 157
Fairness, 124
    and justice, 69, 104, 131, 145
Falsification, 108
Family stakeholders, 94
Farrar, Eleanor, 5, 6, 154
Federal funding, 87, 130, 150
Federal stakeholders, 17ff., 67
Federal support, 16, 23, 55, 58, 60,
    70, 133, 136, 156
Field Foundation, 18, 146
Formalism, 136, 159
Formative evaluation, 61, 74, 78,
    82, 99, 102, 103, 116, 119, 121,
    123, 130, 134, 138, 142, 151, 162
Fund raising. *See* Promotion
Funding, 23, 55, 58, 60, 88, 90, 136,
    156
    strategy, 123

Generalization, x, 32, 34, 72, 110,
    118, 119, 123, 130, 133ff., 149
Glass, Gene, 33, 72, 73
Goals, 80, 94
Gold, Norman, *passim*
Grades, 63, 79, 96, 105, 123
Gradualism. *See* Incremental ethic
Graham, Patricia, 4, 18
Guba, Egon, x
Guttentag, Marcia, 32, 75, 141, 145

Hamilton, David, 134
Hardy, Jimmy, 50, 89, 105
Hastings, Thomas, xi
Havelock, Ronald, 153
Herndon, Enid, 68
Hill, Rigney, 53, 55
Hill, Sue, xi
Horton, Richard, 64, 113
Hostility, 112, 116
House, Ernest, xi, xii, 5, 6, 29, 69,
    76, 84, 145, 147, 154
Houston schools, 8, 13, 15, 97
Humanism, 114
Huron Institute, 5, 33

I.S. 22 (Mott School), 16, 48
Ibsen, Henrick, ix
IDC, 16, 18
Impact
    criteria, 26, 49, 58, 60, 95, 113

Impact (*continued*)
    data, 34, 46, 62ff., 77, 85, 88, 89,
        101, 104, 109, 121, 123, 126,
        129, 139, 159
    evaluation, 99
Implementation, 86
Imprimatur use, 141, 148
Incremental ethic, 26, 35, 56, 65,
    130, 138, 149, 156
Indianapolis schools, *passim*
Information
    feedback, 85, 94, 102
    needs, 29, 30, 35, 40, 46, 69, 82,
        106, 133, 143ff.
    technology, 147
Institutionalization, 35, 60, 61, 74
Instrumentalism, 138
Integrity of evaluation, 126
Intentionality, xii
Interagency collaboration, 36, 59,
    78, 117
Interference, 156
Interpretive method, xi
Intervention, 61, 74, 78, 82
Intrusiveness, evaluator, 27, 38, 75,
    152
Intuitive research, xi, 134
Investments, 11, 62, 73, 96, 111,
    131, 138, 157, 159

Jackson, Jesse, 6, 23, 54, 83, 154
John F. Kennedy School, 139
Jones, William, 110
Julia Richman H.S., 11, 48, 58, 106
Juvenile justice system, 72, 121

Kalp, Karl, 85, 110
Kaplan, Abraham, 160
Kennedy, Mary, x
Klein, Malcolm, xii, 33, 72–79, 85,
    120, 145
Knowledge production, 129, 133ff.
    *See also* Generalization
Koch, Edward, 16, 48, 97, 115
Krug, Robert, 25, 29, 34, 52, 72, 90
Kurtz, Howie, 23

Lance, Bert, 23
Letson, John, 139
Lewis, David, 29, 49, 50, 89, 103,
    112, 145
Light, Richard, 33

Lilly Endowment, 4, 16, 17, 116
Lindblom, Charles, 161
Lipsitz, Paula, 115
Los Angeles schools, 97
*Losing Ground*, 97
Love, Ruth, 13
Lucas, Gregory, 112
Lugar, Richard, 15, 17, 112

Management information, 38, 49,
    100, 107–09, 142, 155
Manipulation, 108
Maxwell, Kathleen, 100, 107
Mays, Benjamin, 17
McConahay, Mary Jane, 145
McCreadie, Jennifer, 72
McGonagill, Grady, 5
McLaughlin, Milbrey, 153
McWilliams, Joyce, xii, 86, 102, 155,
    158
Messianic leadership, 120, 122. *See
    also* Charisma
Meta-evaluation, x, 68, 100, 118,
    120, 148, 162
Mileff, Susan, 53
Milliken, William, *passim*
Mini-experiments, 138
Misrepresentation, 59, 94, 108, 130
Mobility, student, 95
Moore, Alexander, 110
Moses, Kathlyn, 18, 23, 69, 86, 97,
    119
Mott School. *See* I.S. 22
Multiple perspectives, 85, 91, 103,
    110, 156, 160
Murray, Charles, *passim*
Murray, Saundra, 53, 54, 107, 154

NIE, xi, 18, 66ff.
Naturalistic research, x, 46, 72, 134
Negotiations, 85, 87, 143
*New Republic*, 23
New York City schools, 7, 13, 63,
    96, 106, 115, 156
Non-uniformity, 58, 62

Oakland schools, 8, 13, 15, 97
Observation data, 118
Ogilvy and Mather, 16
One-researcher project, 53, 55
Oostdyk, Harold, 5, 11, 16, 17, 59,
    72, 106, 108, 112, 116, 118, 129

Organization, 115, 117, 150, 151
Osborne, John, 23
Outcome measurement. *See* Impact
Outstationing, 83, 87–89, 95, 97, 115
Overby, Dian, 53
Overman, Dean, 18

Paine, Andrew, 112
Parents, 82
Particularism, xii, 71, 134ff., 161
Perloff, Robert, 33, 71–78, 83, 120
Personal behavior, 63, 73
Personalism, 5, 9, 70, 73, 78, 93, 125, 130, 134, 138, 151, 153, 156
Phenomenological study, x, 134
Plankenhorn, Andrew, 64, 113
Polanyi, Michael, 160
Police records, 58, 63–66
Policy research, x, 121, 133, 139, 158
Policy-makers, 83, 132, 141, 149
Political context, 15ff., 55, 70, 87, 88, 113, 119, 129, 132, 148
Portrayal, x, 46, 72
Pregnancy, 46
Problem solving, 46, 134, 136, 149
Process data, 123, 126, 130
Process issues, 94
Productivity, 101, 109, 160
Professional affiliation, 149
Professionalization, 60
Progressive focusing, 26, 56, 60, 151. *See also* Incrementalism
Project Propinquity, 5, 16, 117
Project Talent, 130
Promotion program, 16, 57, 59, 93, 97, 100, 106, 108, 120, 137
Proposal evaluation, 25ff.
Proppe, Oli, xi
Public relations. *See* Promotion
Pure form, 11, 42, 48, 118, 123, 157
PUSH/Excel, 6, 23, 53, 54, 81, 97, 154

Qualitative data, 27, 69, 80
Quality assurance, 44, 77, 95, 99
Quellmalz, Edys, 33, 76, 79, 83
Quieting reform, x, 99, 102, 129, 130, 132, 142, 144, 149ff.

Racism, 108, 110
Rapport, 29, 48, 107, 110, 129, 153

Raudenbush, Stephen, 5
Reactivity, 99, 129, 161. *See also* Quieting reform
Readiness for evaluation. *See* evaluability
Reading scores, 12, 48, 63, 65, 78, 89
Reagan administration, 70, 85, 88, 97, 119, 130, 159
Rebuttal, 61, 85, 86, 90, 94, 102, 111, 121, 150, 152, 155
Redish, Janice, 34, 41, 52, 145
Reed, Ray, 72
Regression analyses, 40, 65
Remediation, 31
Request for proposals, 25ff.
Research questions, 41, 47, 73, 85, 88, 101, 107, 126, 131, 132, 140, 147–61
Resignation, 96
Resolve, 163
Responsive evaluation, x, 67, 145
Rich's Department Store, 97
Rich, Spencer, 70
Richmond, Naomi, xi, 49
Rossi, Peter, 33, 125, 136, 149
Rouse, Victor, 52, 53, 75

Sample attrition, 12, 50, 61
Samuels, Howard, 13, 15, 100, 109, 152–55, 158
Schedule, xiv, 8, 43, 46, 51
Schiller, Jeffrey, 69
Schön, Donald, 134
School goals, 80, 94
Schrank, Peter, 33
Schubert, Jane, 25, 29, 34, 52, 72, 107
Schwartz, Robert, 119
Schwarz, Paul, xii, 25, 29, 34, 44, 53, 56, 96, 138, 139, 192
Scores. *See* Data files
Scriven, Michael, 139
Sechrest, Lee, 33, 76, 79, 124
Services delivery, 35ff., 41, 59, 88, 94, 126, 130
Services integration, 5, 9, 31, 36ff., 41, 57, 59ff., 72, 75, 83–87, 94, 113, 139
Shorthouse Neil, 104
Signaling use, 141, 148
Simons, Toni, 105

Situational factors. *See* Particularism
Smith, Carolyn, 106
Smith, H. S., 5, 48, 50, 89, 97, 114
Smith, Louis, x
Smith, William, 105, 111
Snapper, Kurt, 75
Social agency staffs, 83
Social science, ix, 76, 84, 86, 100, 110, 125, 130, 133–36, 153, 157, 160, 162
Social services, 35, 36, 50, 58, 83, 139
Solution building, 26, 130, 136ff., 149
Sponsors, 14, 17, 23, 137
Spraggins, Bruce, 106
Staff training, 93, 94, 95, 108, 115
Staffing evaluation, 51ff.
Stake, Robert, 33, 38, 40, 64, 71–76, 99, 132, 144
Stakeholder
    concept, x, 4, 5, 27ff., 67, 72, 81, 84, 104, 111, 116, 118, 125
    groups, 46, 60, 62, 76, 81ff., 88, 112, 133, 140, 143ff.
    process, 86, 88, 132
Stalford, Charles, 68, 118
Standardized testing, 123
Standards, 124, 131, 149, 156, 158
Standards & Goals Project, 53
Stanford Consortium, 141, 144
Stern, Stanley, 116
Street academies, 5, 15, 17, 48, 97, 105, 114
Street workers, 91
Student selection. *See* Admissions
Students, 114
Stufflebeam, Daniel, 145
Subjectivity, xi, 34, 102, 134
Summative evaluation, 139
Survival kit, 86, 155

Tacit knowledge, 160
Taylor, Myrtice, xii, 64, 113
Tech 300, 12, 16
Technical assistance, 45, 59, 61, 67, 74. *See also* Formative evaluation

Technical Panel, xiv, 32ff., 61, 71ff., 86, 90, 97, 118, 120ff., 133, 137, 145, 152
Technical quality, 33
Territoriality, 117
Test norms, 79
Testing, 86
Theory building, 139ff. *See also* Generalization
Thompson, J. Walter, 16
Time allocations, 51
Title XX, 12
Trumbull, Deborah, xi, 76, 105, 110, 112, 114, 161
Trust, 29, 60, 103, 104, 110, 153
Tutoring, 107, 123

U.S. Postal Service, 17
UDIS study, xv, 53, 104
Understanding, 141
Uniformity of program, 47, 62, 143, 151
United Way, 89, 117, 159
Unobtrusive measurement, 27, 38, 94
Urban education, 140 and *passim*
Utility of evaluation, 15, 30, 46, 68, 112–19, 127–29, 140ff., 162
Utilization, 34, 40

Validation, 88, 104–06, 107, 112, 118, 124, 126
Von Wright, Georg, 134

Walling, Willoughby, 18, 23, 32
Washington, D.C., schools, 8, 97
*Washington Monthly*, 23
Webb, Eugene, 33, 72, 73, 75, 138
Weiner, Stephen, 144
Weiss, Carol, 5, 142
Whyte, W. F., 158
Wiley, David, 33, 73, 74, 138
Work ethic, 50

Young Life, 17
Youth Research International, 16

Zero-base budgeting, 158
Zimmer, Henry, 89, 117